MILE WIDE, INCH DEEP

Experiencing God Beyond the Shallows,
Soul Care for Busy Pastors and the
Rest of Us

DAVE JACOBS

All scripture quotes are a paraphrase of the author.

ISBN: 1499628447
ISBN 13: 9781499628449

Dedication

It seems customary for a writer to dedicate his first book to his spouse. I will follow in this tradition, not for tradition's sake, but because it is appropriate to do so. The reason for this is that Ellen is such a wonderful wife, mother, and grandmother that I doubt there could ever be too many things dedicated to her. She played an invaluable role in the development of this book. Ellen was my primary editor. No matter how many times I gave her my manuscript, she always had suggestions that made it stronger, clearer, and better. Without her, this book would be a mess of misspellings and grammatical errors, but it would also lack clarity and the wisdom of her observations. I can't remember how many times Ellen told me, "Remember, you're not in a hurry." She forced me to slow down, rethink, rewrite, and thus produce a book that is infinitely better than when it started out.

Ellen, I love you, and I dedicate this book to you.

Special Thanks

I want to thank Craig Simonian for putting the idea for this book in my head, back in 2010. Thanks to all my beta readers who in the middle of their busy lives took the time to help me with this project: Garris Elkins, Marty Boller, Wayne and Sabrina MacQueen, Steve Mason, Steve Summerell, Mike Duran, and Mike McNichols. Thanks to my pastor Garris Elkins who cleared away the fog for me in regard to self-publishing by sharing with me his experiences and pointing me in the direction of CreateSpace.

Contents

Foreword by Bob Logan   ix

Preface   xi

Introduction   xv

1. The Ministry: Enemy of Your Devotional Life?   1

2. Wide Margins   7

3. Detaching from Attachments   15

4. Energy and Equanimity in the Closet   29

5. Contentment in the Closet   37

6. Demystifying Mysticism   49

7. "But What About…?"   55

8. To Monk   61

9. Resistance: When the Enemy Is You   65

10. Sermon Fodder or Soul Food?   71

11. The Love of Sleep   79

12. Spiritual Journaling   85

13. Uncomfortable Reading   93

14. The Required Chapter on Prayer   101

15. They Need a Mystic   109

16. Baby Steps   115

About the Author   129

Notes   131

Foreword by Bob Logan

I've known Dave for a long time; he's a good friend of mine. Because I know him, I'm not surprised to read here about how he engages the pastors he coaches. He intuitively moves the level of discussion down to the deeper things: how we define success, concerns about reputation, the desire for significance, personal ambition, how we compare ourselves with others, the need to be liked, peer approval, boredom and busyness. These under-the-surface concerns have a defining impact on how we engage our pastoral role.

As you read this book, you sense that Dave knows what he's writing about. He gets it on an experiential level. He has also talked with enough other pastors to see the common threads that come into play as pastors keep butting their heads against the same wall. Having been a pastor and having coached pastors, Dave sees the problem of busyness from all sides. He addresses the problem with empathy and helps you feel understood without ever letting you off the hook—for the goal is not to come to terms with our busyness, but to overcome it.

In *Mile Wide, Inch Deep*, Dave outlines practical, doable steps you can take that will result in real changes in your life and ministry. It is possible to have margin in your life, even if you are a pastor. Dave can help you see your way to a different kind of ministry. If you're feeling tired and dry of soul, this book was written for you. Instead of continuing to run yourself ragged, open your arms to embrace the contentment and equanimity that God has for you.

• • •

Dr. Bob Logan is internationally recognized as an authority in church planting, church growth, and leadership development. The author of numerous books and workbooks, Bob's current areas of focus are coaching, speaking, and developing leaders in missional, incarnational contexts. Bob's most recent book is *The Missional Journey*, (ChurchSmart Resources, 2013.)

Preface

Journal entry from May 4, 2010:

> A client of mine, Craig Simonian, e-mailed me encouraging me to write a book. "You could call it 'Soul-care for busy pastors' or something like that," he said.

> Not a bad title. It was nice to know he was thinking of me.

> What could I possibly have to say that hasn't already been said by those who easily know more about the topic than I do? My knowledge and my practice is so elementary. I would have to write about the prayer life I wish I had.

> You write a book and you immediately are thought of as an expert, or at least someone that knows enough about your subject to write about it. Writing a book on soul-care would be like perpetuating an exaggeration about myself.

Actually, I do know a little, but what I know in my head is much bigger in comparison to my experiences and practices.

If my knowledge is elementary school then my practices are in utero. Still…Craig's e-mail was nice. It did make me think: What would I write if I were forced to? Interesting question.

Should I explore this question? It's true, I have no interest whatsoever in writing about anything else. Anything else that I might know pales in comparison. Ellen asked me: What does Craig's e-mail make you think?

Good question. I answered, "It doesn't make me think anything." Which wasn't exactly true. It made me think two things:

1. What a dumb idea.
2. What would I write if I had to?

Someone once said: "God usually gives us questions when He intends to answer them."

• • •

Why the title, *Mile Wide, Inch Deep*?

Humorist Artemus Ward, (a favorite author of US President Abraham Lincoln) estimated the River Platte to be "a mile wide and an inch deep." Many pastors, if they were honest, would say that Ward could have just as easily been describing their own spirituality.

If you feel like your depth of intimacy with God is an inch deep, while your ministry responsibilities stretch you a mile wide, then this book was written for you. I want to help you experience God beyond the shallows. I believe it's possible to go deeper.

I began this book halfway through 2010. I managed to jot down some ideas and write the introduction and then stopped to begin work on another book. I then put that book on hold and returned to this one in 2012.

While fine-tuning the first draft, I realized...this isn't a very long book.

I didn't start out thinking about length (i.e., "I'm going to write a three hundred–page book."); I just started writing and then stopped when I had written what I wanted to say. I've often told my coaching clients that brevity is a virtue. I value brevity. I guess this book was an opportunity to put brevity into practice.

I don't have a lot to say, but I hope what I have to say is enough.

Introduction

I used to be a pastor, but now I'm not. I didn't quit; I retired. When I retired, it felt like I was quitting, but after almost thirty years of ministry, I think you've earned the right to call it retiring. In fact, I think that anyone who stays in the ministry for more than three years should be able to retire with head held high. It's like in the military. They have an honorable or dishonorable discharge. Make it past three years pastoring and you should qualify for an honorable discharge. So in 2006 I retired, and now I coach pastors and church leaders.

I'll bet you've read those articles that report on the alarming number of ministers that quit. One such study said that 1,500 pastors leave the ministry every month. I don't know how that can be true but who am I to argue with these reports? Let me say, however, my surprise is not over how many pastors leave the ministry but over how many actually remain in the ministry.

The late leadership guru Peter Drucker said that "the four hardest jobs in America are: the president of the United States, a university president, a CEO of a hospital, and a pastor."[1]

Pastoring a church is hard, really hard. Everyone agrees it's hard, but there is disagreement as to why it's hard. Some pastors say it would not be so hard if they had more people, more money, more volunteers, more cooperation, more time, more resources. But you know, I think if you had all those things it would still be hard.

"Yes, Dave, but it would be easier."

Maybe.

• • •

I'm into my eighth year of coaching pastors. This is my full-time job. It's all I do. I've been asked if there is anything they all have in common: a common problem, something true regardless of denomination, church size, or age of the pastor. I always answer the same way: "Most pastors are overworked, underpaid, and don't take care of their souls." In my coaching practice, I address all three. The purpose of this book is to discuss "soul-care" for the busy pastor but to do so in such a way that it will also prove helpful to the rest of us non-pastor types.

There's a reason why you picked up this book. Something in the title or the subject matter touched a place in your heart. You've read the books on church growth and leadership. You know what it means for someone to be postmodern, purpose-driven, seeker-sensitive, emergent, and missional. What you lack is not information but *formation*. A wise person once said, "You teach what you know but you reproduce what you are."

It's who you are on the inside that interests you, or concerns you. Don't you wish you were more deeply spiritual? Something keeps reminding you that your personal intimacy with Jesus is the most important thing, but there are so many other things that pull you in the opposite direction. There is the person you are and the person you want to be, and you wish you could close that gap. You can. This book is about closing the gap.

I believe this is the right time for you to read this book. Maybe you'll hear some things you've never heard before. Maybe you'll read old things in a new way, made new by the Spirit who wants to help you be and experience all the Father wants you to be and experience.

In the prologue to Pope Francis's book, *Open Mind, Faithful Heart*, José María Arancedo writes that some books, "[ask] of us an unhurried, reflective reading. The first requirement for advancing in something important is to give ourselves sufficient time. We are accustomed to reading rapidly in order to stay informed and up to date, but this book has a very different purpose."[2]

Please read this book slowly. The slower you read it the more you will benefit from it. Fight the temptation to rush through it. At the end of each chapter you'll find some questions for reflection and journaling. Find a nice, comfortable place to sit and be alone with God and each chapter. Invite the Holy Spirit to help you think and process what you've read. During your time of reflection you will begin to notice things rising to the surface, thoughts coming to you. Write them down. Don't worry too much about grammar. Let these ideas and impressions travel from your head to your heart, down your arm, through your hand, out your pen, and onto the paper.

Remember that "gap" I mentioned just a moment ago? It can close. It will take a lifetime, but it can close little by little. I believe this process was well underway in your heart before you bought this book. The things you are about to read are links in your long chain of getting to know God more intimately. Let's begin.

one

The Ministry:
Enemy of Your Devotional Life?

If an obvious enemy was attacking me I could understand it, or someone who blatantly hated me, then I could avoid them. But what surprised me was when the attack came from someone I did not expect, from a companion and friend.

Ps. 55:12

Mike was about eight months into his church plant when we began to meet. One of the opening questions I asked him was, "What took you by surprise?"

"I didn't expect it to be this hard," he replied. "Coming up with a sermon every week is more difficult than I imagined. I thought people would be more committed than they are. But you know what really surprised me?"

"Tell me," I said eagerly.

1

"I didn't anticipate the hit my devotional life would take. For some reason I thought it would be easier once I was in the ministry to be close to God. My quiet times were actually better before I started the church."

"Mike," I responded, glad we were having this discussion over the phone so he couldn't see my grin, "can I tell you something you might be surprised to hear?"

"Sure," he said.

"The ministry is ideally designed to sabotage your spiritual life. I might go as far as to say that the ministry can be an enemy to your devotional life."

There was about a five-second pause and then Mike asked, "How do you mean?"

• • •

Mike is not alone. More than one pastor has told me they had a more consistent prayer life before they entered the ministry. The pastorate can undermine our spiritual formation. There are two reasons why this is so.

First of all, most pastors are too busy.

Life for too many leaders is a blur of activity and planning, with sparse occasions for reflection, replenishing, rejoicing, and responding to the relationship the Lord is inviting them to experience and enjoy with Him. The *urgent* crowds out the *essential. Doing* ignores *being. Developing skills* becomes more important than *shaping character.*[3]

My friend, Steve Summerell, was a Vineyard pastor for twenty-five years and is now a spiritual director. His doctoral dissertation was titled "Overcoming Obstacles to Spiritual Formation in the Lives of Vineyard Pastors." Steve's research concluded that the number one obstacle for pastors was busyness.[4] My experience tells me that Steve's findings hold true regardless of denominational affiliation or church size.

Our fifty- and sixty-hour workweeks leave us tired and drained. Too much activity leads to too little time for sitting alone with God. Listen to what that great pastor to pastors, Eugene Peterson, has to say:

> The word *busy* is the symptom not of commitment but of betrayal. It is not devotion but defection. The adjective *busy* set as a modifier to *pastor* should sound to our ears like *adulterous* to characterize a wife or *embezzling* to describe a banker. It is an outrageous scandal, a blasphemous affront....How can I lead people into the quiet place beside the still waters if I am in perpetual motion?
>
> ...The trick, of course, is to get to the calendar before anyone else does. I mark out the times for prayer, for reading, for leisure, for the silence

and solitude out of which creative work—prayer, preaching, and listening—can issue.[5]

Second, it's not just that we're too busy—we're too busy doing good, spiritual things, and those spiritual things can fool us. We study the Bible for the sermons we preach. We do pastoral counseling. We visit people in the hospital. We pray for people. We plan and participate in outreach events for our community. This is what we do. It's all good and fine, but we must remember that *doing* spiritual things is different than *being* spiritual. We can draw just enough spiritual nutrients from the things we do to keep us alive, but not enough for the depth of intimacy with Jesus that is necessary for us to be the leaders and pastors our people so desperately need us to be. You can be drowning but think you are swimming. And oftentimes it is those spiritual things that occupy our week, which fool us into thinking we are swimming.

Henri Nouwen warns, "The Evil One would prefer to distract us and fill every little space with things to do, people to meet, business to accomplish, products to be made."[6]

Richard Foster adds, "If we are constantly being swept off our feet with frantic activity, we will be unable to be attentive at the moment of inward silence."[7]

We will return to the topic of busyness in chapter 2, but for now, here are some questions for quiet reflection:

1. Is my spiritual life better or worse since I entered the ministry?

2. Is my spiritual life better or worse since this time last year?

3. Are there ways in which my ministry responsibilities are sabotaging my spiritual formation?

4. Have I been confusing spiritual tasks (ministry stuff) with spiritual depth?

5. What adjustments could I make to my calendar that would insure an adequate amount of time to be alone with God?

6. How will I evaluate the state of my spiritual life?

two

Wide Margins

I have to work hard at bringing my will under the control of the Holy Spirit. I don't want to succeed in my ministry but fail in my Christianity.

1 Cor. 9:27

In his book *Five Smooth Stones for Pastoral Work*, Eugene Peterson writes, "In order for there to be conversation and prayer that do the pastoral work of meeting the intimacy needs among people, there must be a wide margin of quiet leisure that defies the functional, technological, dehumanizing definitions that are imposed upon people by others in the community."[8]

Remember that phrase: "a wide margin of quiet leisure."

Having interacted with many pastors in North America and around the world, I have observed that most of those in the ministry are too busy. There is simply no time for the wide margin of quiet leisure that

Peterson speaks of. Because of this, many pastors feel tired, stressed, and spiritually dry.

How can we lead others into deep waters if we ourselves live in the shallows created by constant activity? Few people are more constantly active than the average pastor.

The pastor's week is filled with phone calls, follow-up meetings, mentoring, e-mails, sermonizing, problem solving, people placating, visitation, vision-casting, drop-ins, counseling, planning, dodging bullets, and putting out fires.

Richard Foster comments in *Celebration of Discipline*, "In contemporary society our Adversary majors in three things: noise, hurry, and crowds. If he can keep us engaged in 'muchness' and 'manyness,' he will rest satisfied. Psychiatrist Carl Jung once remarked, 'Hurry is not *of* the Devil; it *is* the Devil.'"[9]

Great pastors are organized, focused, and productive without the sense of being driven, hurried, or busy.

A. W. Tozer suggests, "Our religious activities should be ordered in such a way as to leave plenty of time [margin] for the cultivation of the fruits of solitude and silence."[10]

Henri Nouwen dares to ask, "Is there a space in your life [margin] where the Spirit of God has a chance to speak or act or show up? To be contemplative means to peel off the blindfolds that keep us from seeing his coming in us and around us. It means to learn to listen in the spaces of quiet [margin] we leave for God and thereby know how better to relate to the world around us."[11]

Can you think of any good things you could take off your plate in order to make margin for better things, such as spiritual formation, thinking and planning, and cultivating key relationships? Notice, I said *good* things.

For most of us the challenge is not to take *bad* things off our plate. Bad things are obvious; they prick our conscience. What push us over the edge are good things that crowd out better things. Our calendars are not filled with too much bad, but with too much good.

God will give me all the time I need to do the things He wants me to do. *Too busy* is an indication that there is something in my life that did not originate from God.

Here are six steps I follow to break free from too busy and create wide margins.

Step One: Stop, face it, and admit that I am too busy.

I can't allow myself to see too busy on my calendar or feel too busy in my life and blow it off. I dare not minimize it. I can't add too busy to my to-do list and deal with it tomorrow, or the next day, or next month, or next year…when things calm down. Things never calm down.

Stop. Deal with it now. You will remain too busy if you delay dealing with too busy.

Step Two: Look at my calendar.

Consider the past three to four weeks. Make a list of all the things I am doing or have to do on a regular basis that add up to too busy.

Step Three: Identify how many things on my list are responsibilities clearly given to me from God.

Now, mark those items with a G. Next, how many things on my list are not clearly given to me from God? Mark those things with an NG. Finally, how many items on my list am I not sure of? Mark those items with an NSO. Don't just think about it; actually write it all down.
Step Four: Look for things on my list that I could, or should, stop giving my time to.

Some things need to be abandoned and some things need to be delegated. Be courageous and abandon what needs to be abandoned. Begin the process to delegate what needs to be delegated.

I know, often this is easier said than done…but start the process. You can do it. It will take time. It will not be easy, but you can do it.

Step Five: Ask God to open up my calendar when I am facing a particularly overbooked week.

It's not unusual for me to have five coaching appointments a day. I always schedule a half hour between calls, but still, that's five hours on the phone a day. My problem isn't that I don't have the time for five, the problem is that whoever is number five doesn't get me at my best. I'm simply more tired by my fifth call.

So, because I want to be at my best for the men and women I talk to, when I know a five-call day coming up I ask God for "divine appointment cancellations." Sometimes He answers my prayers...and sometimes not. The principle is: if you are facing a week that is too busy, ask for divine appointment cancellations.

Step Six: Ask the Holy Spirit to show me, in advance, the commitments I'm about to take on that will result in being too busy.

Great leaders say no a lot. They also say yes a lot; but in regards to their calendar in order to prevent themselves from being too busy, they say no a lot. It's easier to say no in advance than it is to say no later after having said yes. Ask the Holy Spirit to help you recognize when to say no in advance.

• • •

There must be a margin, a space between me and the world, between me and my ministry, between me and my regular, day-to-day life. Once I find that margin I will discover that this margin is the *real life*...more life than the life it separates me from. The margin is where life is experienced, and once margin happens I'm in a better place to cross back over into the pseudo-life. In fact, the margin brings life to life—color, fragrance, texture, and sound. It's like the difference between a picture of a beautiful forest and actually walking through one. I must create more margin in my life and more space in my heart.

A deep spirituality is the only hope I have to break free from the things that do me little good, and instead cultivate discontent, friction, frustration, and shallowness of soul. Times of retreat and reflection (that "wide margin of quiet leisure") provide the space necessary to be who I want to be, who my people need me to be, and who God desires me to be.

Questions for reflection:

1. Do I have enough margin in my life?

2. How much would be enough?

3. What comes to my mind when I think of "a wide margin of quiet leisure?"

4. What good things could I take off my plate in order to make room for better things?

5. What would have to happen in order for me to take those things off my plate?

6. Who might be able to help me create more margin in my life?

three

Detaching from Attachments

Don't let me get stuck in the muck.
Ps. 69:14a

Detachment is an interesting word, and one with many meanings.

Detachment can refer to being objective or aloof. Detachment can speak of a military group of troops. Detachment can mean a group of people separated from a larger group of people. Detachment can mean the separation of an object from something it was previously attached to. And...

Detachment can refer to the action or process of separating yourself from something in order to reduce anxiety or stress. In psychology this is called *emotional detachment.*

If I were a psychologist who worked with people in the ministry, I think that nine times out of ten, the anxiety, stress, and lack of fulfillment pastors would bring to me could be traced back to a need for emotional (or spiritual) detachment.

Here are my top seven things pastors and church leaders need to be detached from. Each one of these are interrelated—they overlap and feed each other.

1. Pastors need to be detached from **reputation**.

I'm not talking about having a good reputation. We all want to be leaders with integrity and character.

Sometimes I wonder what friends and family will say about me after I'm gone. The word *eulogy* comes from the Latin (eulogium) and means *high praise*. Will I have high praise, low praise, or no praise? I'm hoping for the best. We'll see.

But there's a difference between wanting to have a good reputation and needing to have a good reputation in order to feel good about yourself and your ministry. We need to be detached from the *need* to have a good reputation. I think we can care too much what other people think of us, especially our peers and supervisors, and that much of this need can be traced back to our insecurity and pride.

2. Pastors need to be detached from **numbers**.

There's nothing wrong with counting. Have you noticed all the counting that took place in Bible times? In fact, there's a book in the Bible called Numbers.

When I was pastoring I had to count dollars. I just couldn't show up to the bank and hand them the offering and say, "Here...do something with this."

There is also nothing inherently wrong with counting heads (attendance). There can be some advantages to keeping attendance records. However, if I find myself feeling "up" when the numbers are up and "down" when the numbers are down, I just might be too attached to numbers.

Remember, the only thing attendance numbers tell me for certain are how many people were sitting out there staring back at me. Counting heads tells me nothing about what is going on inside of my people, nor does it tell me what type of impact my people are having for Jesus in their neighborhoods, workplace, and in their other networks of relationships.

But there's a difference between wanting to have a numerically growing church and *needing* to have a numerically growing church in order to feel good about yourself and your ministry. We need to be detached from the need to have a numerically growing church.

3. Pastors need to be detached from **success**.

Now, of course, all of this is dependent upon one's definition of success. Unfortunately, the Western Church defines success almost exclusively by numbers (e.g., how many were in attendance, and how much was in the offering).

There were times when I didn't look forward to hanging out with pastors because I knew that eventually someone was going to ask me, "So...how are things going at your church?" This question is usually the way one pastor finds out if he or she is more or less successful than another pastor.

If my church was growing (which was seldom), then I didn't mind answering their question. If my church was not growing (which was often), I looked for a way to change the subject or leave the room.

It didn't matter how many good things were happening in my church, I didn't really feel *successful* if my church was in decline or had plateaued for a long period of time. Someone could have been raised from the dead and I'd be thinking, "That's nice, but that church down the street, the one that is bigger than us, they're more successful than we are."

I like to challenge pastors to sit down with their leaders and discover ways to define success in their church that have very little relation to size or numbers.

But there's a difference between wanting to have success and needing to have success in order to feel good about yourself and your church. We need to detach from the need to be thought of as successful.

4. Pastors need to be detached from **peer acknowledgment and approval**.

It feels good to have a peer—whether it's a fellow pastor or denominational supervisor—tell you you're doing a great job. But this seldom happens unless, of course, your church is growing.

"So, Bob, how are things going at your church?"
"Well…our numbers have been about the same for the past three years."
"Are you kidding me? Why, that's fantastic! I can't believe what a good and faithful pastor you are. How about you speak at our next regional conference?"

Never gonna happen.

There's nothing wrong with wanting to have peer acknowledgment and approval, but needing peer acknowledgment and approval in order to feel positive about yourself and your ministry is a recipe for frustration and disappointment.

Remind yourself: "I am not invisible to God."

The Father sees and appreciates the hard work and sacrifices you, and your family, make in order to be faithful to your call to ministry. You are not invisible.

5. Pastors need to be detached from **personal ambition**.

Personal ambition is an illness of soul where one only feels good about oneself, or worthy in the eyes of God or man, when one is constantly accomplishing and achieving.

Kent Carlson and Mike Lueken in *Renovation of the Church: What Happens When a Seeker Church Discovers Spiritual Formation,* have an entire chapter devoted to ambition in the hearts of pastors. Here are a few quotes from their book:

> It is personal ambition that drives the machinery of "success" in the church context.

> Ambition is often fueled by the insatiable desire to be recognized as important.

> Personal ambition is a ravenous monster not easily tamed. And it is time to admit to each other that it runs rampant in the religious subculture of our day.[12]

It's easier to convince myself that my ambition is holy than it is for me to actually have holy ambition. Three out of the five times the word *ambition* appears in the New Testament it is spoken of negatively. Here are the five verses:

Positive
It should be our ambition, wherever we find ourselves, to be pleasing to Him (2 Cor. 5:9).

Positive
If you want to have a good ambition, let it be to lead a quiet life, mind your own business, and be a good worker. Didn't we tell you this? (1 Thess. 4:11).

Negative
There are some in the ministry motivated by selfish ambition rather than from pure motives... (Phil. 1:17).

Negative
But if you are jealous and selfishly ambitious in your heart, be careful, you don't want to also be arrogant and lie against the truth (James 3:14).

Negative
For where you find jealousy and selfish ambition, you will also find disorder and all kinds of evil (James 3:16).

I need to be brave enough to prayerfully ask God to show me if I need to be detached from ambition. Maybe I need an ambition to be detached from ambition?

6. Pastors need to be detached from **feelings of insignificance**.

I remember a few years after Ellen and I planted our first church in Southern California, we took a trip back to our hometown of San Jose, California, and I lined up a lunch appointment with one of my old college professors, Jim Crain. Back in those days Jim was the "cool professor." He had long hair (long for a man his age working for a relatively conservative Christian college), played the guitar, and wrote contemporary Christian music. He even had his own Christian rock station (Star Song Radio)—cool, right?

I can't remember what Jim and I talked about that day. I must have been whining to him about how hard pastoring was, or how things hadn't worked out like I had planned, or something about feeling insignificant. But what I do remember was one sentence from Jim, a simple principle that I would remember for the rest of my life. Jim looked at me from across the table and said, "Dave, we must learn to embrace apparent insignificance."

Of course, the key word in Jim's sentence was *apparent*. No one is insignificant in the eyes of God. No one's church is insignificant in the eyes of God. You might *feel* insignificant, someone might even incite you to feel insignificant, and that church down the road that is bigger than yours might make your church seem insignificant in comparison—but those feelings are telling you a lie. It's just apparent insignificance, not real insignificance. There are no insignificant people or ministries in the eyes of God.

Believe it or not, next to Jesus, my favorite character in the New Testament is Jesus's cousin, John the Baptist. John is a perfect example of someone willing to embrace apparent insignificance.

Before Jesus came on the scene John was in the spotlight. His ministry was thriving, people were coming from all over to hear him speak and be baptized in his church. Then someone new showed up: Jesus.

Immediately John began to embrace apparent insignificance. John was losing followers; he was giving his blessing to his leadership team to join Jesus. And then he actually came out and said it, one of the most powerful sentences recorded in the Bible: "He must get bigger and I must get smaller." (John 3:30).

John must have thought, "Well, it's over. My ministry is done. It's time for me to fade into obscurity."

Insignificance or apparent insignificance? I say apparent. Consider what Jesus said about his cousin, "No woman has ever given birth to someone more important than John." (Luke 7:28).

There's a difference between wanting to fulfill God's call for my life and needing to feel a significance gained by either comparing my accomplishments to someone else's or by using some other criteria of measurement placed on me by my colleagues, my culture, or my denomination.

I must be willing to appear insignificant in the eyes of others while peacefully resting in the significance I have in the eyes of God. Like our friend John, I must be willing to get smaller, and smaller, and smaller, until I disappear completely into my Father's presence where I am always known, always loved, always appreciated, always significant.

7. Pastors need to be detached from **the need to be liked**.

One of the most common things I run into in my coaching practice is "pastoral intimidation." By this I don't mean the pastor intimidating his/her parishioners, although there's plenty of that, but members of the congregation intimidating the pastor. It's a subtle thing that is hard for the pastor to recognize, let alone admit.

Many pastors avoid confrontation for fear of the ramifications. I don't blame them. In some churches a confrontation with the church board can result in the pastor getting fired. If Aunt Suzie is an influential member of the church you'd better not ruffle her feathers or there will be a price to pay. We want to grow our church, not shrink it, so we strive to keep people happy. If in our attempt to lead we step on people's toes or offend people, they might leave the church and take their money and help with them. In a church that is struggling financially (and many are in this category) and for a pastor who is barely making enough to live on (and there are many in this category), losing people can lead to having your salary cut. Once again, these are legitimate concerns that I've experienced in the past so I certainly don't fault a pastor for having them.

The problem with all of this is that the pastor is leading out of fear and intimidation, which is a nearly impossible way to lead. Pastors can become people-pleasers. They may avoid rocking the boat at any cost. They know what needs to be said or what needs to be done but, due to intimidation and their need to be liked, they may stop being able to act, and instead become paralyzed.

Unless we detach from the need to be liked we will never lead the way the Father wants us to lead, and we will never be released to move freely in our own soul and ministry. Until we stop needing the approval of our people, our board, and Aunt Suzie, we will remain frustrated as pastors, and the Father's will for our church will be frustrated, as well.

Detachment from the need to be liked will take courage. True, we must pick our battles wisely, but to think that we can pastor without a fight, or without taking a hit, is unrealistic.

• • •

Let's remember which definition of detachment we're considering.

Detachment: the action or process of separating yourself from something in order to reduce anxiety or stress.

Once I detach from reputation, numbers, success, peer acknowledgement and approval, personal ambition, feelings of insignificance, and the need to be liked, I will be in a better position to attach to the life-giving, truth-based, healthy things I need to be attached to.

Attachment to God by focusing on personal spiritual formation makes it easier to detach from the things that do me no good.

Questions for reflection:

1. Of the seven things listed above (reputation, numbers, success, peer acknowledgment and approval, personal ambition, feelings of insignificance, and the need to be liked), which one do I need to be detached from the most?

2. How did I become attached to this in the first place?

3. What steps do I need to take in order for me to detach myself from this?

four

Energy and Equanimity
in the Closet

*When it's time to pray, imagine yourself
going into a closet and closing the door.
Find a secret, quiet place to spend time
with your Father. He'll meet you there.*

Matt. 6:6

Since I coach pastors it should come as no surprise
to you that among my list of current clients there
are always a handful that have just about had it with
the ministry. They've tried everything they've been
told to do by the "experts" to have a growing and
healthy church but nothing works. Maybe they've
been shackled to a dysfunctional board that opposes
them or sabotages their pastoral leadership. Their
spouse may be just as close to throwing in the towel
as they are.

The tenacity of pastors never fails to amaze me. Sure, we hear about pastors who quit—sometimes this is the wisest thing to do—but most hang in there, and hang in there, and hang in there...until, for some, they and their family have been whittled away to nothing.

As a coach, it's not my main job to advise, instead my job is to help the people I coach to think, process, and discover on their own what the Father is saying to them. In over seven years of pastoral coaching there have only been two times I've actually told pastors I thought they needed to pack their bags and leave their church rather than stay and try to tough it out. Both times they left. Both times they ended up being glad they did.

Usually when I can see that the pastor has been frustrated and discouraged for a long time, I ask him or her one simple question:

"If nothing changes, how long can you last?"

This question brings up the issue of energy, equanimity, and contentment. We'll focus on contentment in the next chapter but at this point let me ask you, "Do you have enough energy, and equanimity (i.e., mental calmness, composure, and evenness of temper, especially in a difficult situation), to keep going if nothing changes?"

There is only one thing that concerns me more than needing to ask a pastor this question and that is needing to ask this question when the pastor has admitted to me that his or her soul is weak and dry.

You see, it is not an exaggeration to say that most pastors do not have a consistent and meaningful devotional life. What I have found is that energy, equanimity, and contentment in the ministry will occur in direct proportion to the consistency and meaningfulness of the pastor's time alone with God.

Energy and equanimity are found in the closet. Jesus advised, "Go into your prayer closet. Close the door tight. Pray to your Father who is in secret" (Matt. 6:6).

Notice the verbs Jesus used: Go. Close. Pray.

Many pastors seldom go. Some pastors go, but they don't close—leaving their door open to all kinds of distractions. Some pastors go and close, but their prayers always center on their ministry. Rather than a "me alone with God" time, it's more a "me and God and my church" time.

Of course pastors need to pray for their church. However, ministry-related prayers will not result in the personal energy and equanimity needed to remain faithful to the hard work of pastoring. What is my advice?

Don't let the church into your closet. The closet is for you and God. And by that I don't mean you the pastor, but rather you the child of God. The Father wants to spend time with you and whisper words of love and guidance to you. Intercede for your church some other time, some other place, but not in your closet.

Did you notice how many times I've repeated the words *energy* and *equanimity*? I hope so, because they're important.

Energy relates to our physical body.
Equanimity relates to our mind.

• • •

Do you lack energy?

Many pastors tell me that they lack energy. A lack of energy can also feel like a lack of motivation, endurance, or a stick-to-it-ness. They might even admit that they feel physically tired or fatigued.

It's no wonder that some of us lack energy when you consider how often we eat junk, and are overweight. Few of us exercise. We work too many hours and get too little sleep. We don't take enough time off. Constant discouragement and criticism, which often accompany the ministry, drain our energy.

And while some of us are starting to simply feel the effects our age has on our energy, others of us may be suffering regrets from our past and/or fears for our future that suck energy out of us. One of the symptoms of clinical depression is a lack of energy. And certain illnesses such as anemia, thyroid disorder, hypotension (low blood pressure), can all contribute to fatigue.

I don't want to seem naïve or simplistic. I know that the closet, in and of itself, is no guaranteed answer for all of these feelings. However, I believe our closet will affect, and sometimes correct, many of these symptoms. How?

In the closet you might find the power and self-control to be more disciplined with what you eat. In the closet you might be able to discover why you use food inappropriately. In the closet you might find help to be more physically active. In the closet you might discover the faith needed to stop putting in so many hours for the church and therefore trust God to do His part—which is always bigger than your part in maintaining your ministry.

In the closet you will find peace, and peace might affect how well you sleep. Discouragement and criticism will be easier to bear as you draw closer to Jesus in the closet. Regrets and fear are released in the closet. And as far as concerns like clinical depression and the physical ailments listed above, I believe they should be addressed by a combination of the closet *and* the doctor.

Do you lack equanimity?

I don't think I'd ever heard of the word *equanimity* before writing this chapter. Instead of *equanimity*

I would have used words like *calm, level-headedness, serenity,* and *tranquility*—all of which define the word *equanimity.*

The test of equanimity lies in its context.

It's easy to be calm and tranquil when everything is going right, your church is growing, everyone is on board with you, and morale is high. But the real test is to keep your head on straight when your ministry seems to be spinning out of control.

If it is normal for you to be calm, serene, and tranquil regardless of your circumstances, then you have equanimity. Be honest with yourself. Does the word *equanimity* accurately describe you? If not, you're not alone. Most pastors would not score high on equanimity.

Your equanimity will be in direct proportion to the consistency and meaningfulness of your times of solitude with God. In your closet, in that peaceful place, the Father of peace waits for you. There is no guarantee that the closet will change your outward circumstances, but you can count on finding inner peace and calm. In the closet there is equanimity.

Before we turn to the topic of contentment in the closet, here are some questions for reflection:

1. If nothing changes, how long can I last?

2. On a scale of one to ten (ten being high), how would I score my current energy for ministry?

3. On a scale of one to ten (ten being high), how would I score my current joy in ministry?

4. On a scale of one to ten (ten being high), how would I score my current equanimity?

5. What one thing could I do to raise my score by one point?

five

Contentment in the Closet

I have very few needs. One of the reasons for this is that I've learned to be content no matter what life throws at me.

Phil. 4:11

Are you content?

Contentment refers to the peace, acceptance, and joy you have in the ministry even if your church is small, even if your church has plateaued, even if your church is in decline. Contentment will be in direct proportion to the consistency and meaningfulness of your times of solitude with God.

It seems to me that contentment is a big issue for most pastors. And it's no wonder, because there are so many reasons why contentment in the ministry is so elusive.

It's hard to be content in the ministry because we're trying to produce results that are hard to measure. We say we want to make disciples but how do we know when we've made one? What does a disciple look like? We typically only see our people one or maybe two days a week. We don't know what they're like at work, at home, or on vacation. So how do we really know if we are making disciples? We could follow them around snapping pictures like the paparazzi or install secret surveillance cameras at their main hangouts, but that's cost prohibitive, creepy, and we'd probably end up getting punched or arrested. I'm not suggesting that there is no way for us to measure discipleship; I'm just saying it's difficult.

It's hard to be content in the ministry because there is always someone whose church seems to be doing better. The pastor of 50 people lives in the shadow of the pastor of 150, who lives next door to the pastor of 250, who drives past the church of 550 or 5000. Bottom line: contentment cannot be based on comparison because there will always be someone more successful than you.

It's hard to be content in the ministry because there is a constant flow of new ideas, and "the latest thing." Subscribe to any of the popular ministry magazines, such as *Outreach Magazine, Leadership Journal,* or *Charisma,* and you'll find page after page of articles, products, and interviews with successful pastors telling you how they did it and what to try next, and promising church growth as if it were as easy as waving a magic wand. New ideas don't always foster contentment, and if you lack the resources to try the latest thing, or if you have tried it and it didn't work for you, then you are left feeling the opposite of contentedness.

It's hard to be content in the ministry because we're worried that contentment will lead to complacency—or that those we serve will mistake our contentment for complacency. There is a false idea that contentment is synonymous with complacency.

Contentment is a state of peaceful happiness and satisfaction with a certain level of achievement. A content person is not always wishing for more.

Complacency often refers to a smugness or uncritical satisfaction with oneself or one's achievements. When I think of someone who is complacent I imagine them as someone who feels no need to "get off the couch" of life or ministry.

Paul told Timothy, "Godliness coupled with contentment is very beneficial" (1 Tim. 6:4).

God wants you to be content with the size of your church without becoming complacent in regards to discipleship and evangelism. I realize this is not an easy balance to achieve but it is one that must be achieved.

Would you describe your current attitude in regard to the size of your church as "a state of peaceful happiness?" Could you say you are "satisfied with a certain level of achievement, not wishing for more?" Remember, we're talking about the size of your church, not how well your church is doing in reaching the lost, feeding the poor and making serious followers of Christ. Are you content in being the pastor of your church regardless of its size? Can you embrace contentedness without becoming complacent about all the other things the church is supposed to be and do? I hope so. I also know, from personal experience, how hard it is to be content with the size of your congregation.

Is it just me or does it seem like the church-related books pastors read, the conferences they go to, and the ministerial meetings they attend often end up causing them to feel more discontent than content?

There still exists in "Churchianity" far too much emphasis upon numbers and church growth. I'm not against numbers or church growth, but I am against anything that makes pastors feel like they don't measure up.

A content pastor still cares about reaching people and fulfilling the Great Commission. A content pastor puts in a good day's work but refuses to work more hours for the church than is healthy for his or her soul, marriage, and family. It takes courage to be a content pastor because occasionally you will have to dig in your heels and say no to members of your church that want to push you to do more and more and more. There must be some lazy pastors out there but I've never met one. We must find a way to be content without being complacent. It's one thing to want your church to grow and another thing to need your church to grow in order to feel good about yourself and your church. The pastor who does not need his or her church to grow will experience peace, joy, freedom, and contentment.

It's hard to be content in the ministry because the driven, type A personality (a temperament marked by excessive competitiveness and ambition, as well as an obsession with accomplishing tasks quickly) is rewarded in our culture. And, if you don't have a type A personality you can feel like a slacker or someone destined for mediocrity.

Yes, you've got to have some drive or else nothing will ever get done. But, on the other hand, I know many pastors who are too driven, and they're driving themselves to an early grave. It's hard to be content with your pedal to the floor.

It's hard to be content in the ministry because our culture narrowly defines success using three words: *bigger*, *more*, or *new*. Therefore, if your ministry or church seems smaller, less, or old, you are not viewed as successful. This cultural definition, of which few of us can escape, contributes to our discontent. It is ingrained in all of us to want to be successful.

I've recommended this book for years: *Rethinking the Successful Church* by Samuel D. Rima. This book isn't on my "recommended" reading list, it's on my "read this book or go to jail" list. Every pastor or future pastor who hasn't already read Rima's book should stop what they're doing right now and find this book, order this book, beg, borrow, or steal this book.

Most pastors, if they're really honest—really, really, really honest—would admit that they would love to be thought of as having a successful church. This isn't necessarily bad if one's definition of success is a pure one, unaffected by our western culture. But as Rima points out: "The task of redefining our understanding of success will not be an easy one. Over the course of a lifetime we have had drilled into us a cultural view of success that is not easy to shake."[13]

The word *success* has become so Americanized that it is hard to use it without thinking of words like *size, numbers, big, popular,* and *influential.* I'd like to throw out the word *success,* at least any connection between it and the local church, and replace it with the word *value.* "For me, success in ministry has become much more qualitative than it is quantitative. The reality is that it is entirely possible to manufacture phenomenal church growth and produce dramatic tangible indicators of success, while at the same time accomplish nothing of any genuine eternal value."[1415]

I agree with Rima that we live in a culture of success, and I would add that today's Christian culture tends to define success in the same way our secular culture does. Equating size with success has been drilled into us over the course of our life time. Let's throw out the word 'success' and replace it with the word 'value.'

You and your church may never be successful according to the world's definition but that doesn't mean you don't have value. A church can have value whether it has only five, fifty, or a hundred members. "At some point on our ministry journey we have got to realize that we can build the biggest church in the world and actually see thousands of people coming to Christ, and still be an abysmal failure in the eyes of God. If our motives are impure, our methods dubious, and our personal character and spirituality seriously flawed, I do not believe God considers us successful."[16]

You have value when you remain faithful to your calling even when it would be easier to pull a Jonah and run in the opposite direction. You have value when you show up week after week to teach the Word. You have value when you love your people—especially those who are hard to love. You have value when you try to produce followers of Jesus, when you pray for people, when you counsel people, when you comfort people who are in pain. Your church might not have success, but it does have value when it loves those inside and outside its doors.

Throw out success. Replace it with value.

Paul said that it is required of ministers that we be found trustworthy, not successful (1 Cor. 4:2). Mother Teresa is reported to have said, "God has not called you to be successful. God has called you to be faithful."

I know everyone has heard of the famous billion-aire John D. Rockefeller. In an interview, when asked, "How many more dollars until you're satisfied?" Mr. Rockefeller answered, "Just one more."

We pastors aren't much different: the pastor of twenty-five parishioners dreams of the day when he will have fifty; the pastor of fifty dreams of the day when she will have a hundred; the pastor of a hundred dreams of the day when the church membership will rise above two hundred. But once you pass two hundred, you dream of five hundred. The dreaming goes on and on and on. It's all a dream: the dream that at some point, at some size, you will feel successful. You won't. You will always dream of "just one more."

Since we've been brainwashed into believing that success in the ministry means bigger, more, and new—and since there will always be a bigger, bigger; a more, more; and a newer new—it's no wonder we find it hard to be content.

Finally, it's hard to be content in the ministry because we can get bored with the routines that make up pastoring.

If you are like most pastors, your week is usually made up of the same things. You prepare sermons, counsel, plan, visit, run meetings with teams, occasion-ally marry and bury, return calls or e-mails, dodge bul-lets, and put out fires. This is what you do. You do it every week, week after week, year after year.

Pastoring is not complicated, but it is hard. One of the hardest things about pastoring is accepting the routines of ministry. Over time we can get bored. We might not recognize it as boredom at first, but that's what it is, and that's why some of us find ourselves discontent.

Luckily, many of the things we routinely do will get our adrenaline pumping, but not everything that makes up ministry is exciting. This is especially true if you've been pastoring for a long time.

Can I digress slightly and say a few things about boredom and the ministry?

1. Some people, because of the way they are wired, are bored more easily than others. If this is you this doesn't mean you're bad, it just means you're bored.

2. Feeling bored can be a symptom of something deeper within us that needs to be explored. There is usually a reason why we feel bored and often that reason is unknown to us. It's helpful to bring our feelings of boredom to God in quiet reflection asking Him to show us if our boredom is symptomatic of something else.

Let me give you a personal example. I've been bored in the past only to discover that at the root of my boredom was impatience with people, or—impatience with God. It seems like both God and people are slow. Discipleship takes time. Growing a healthy church is slow work. Trying to implement change is a really, really slow process. Think how slowly Christ is formed in you.

God has a plan, and God has a pace, and that pace is often slower than we would like. Because of this, we get impatient; and because of that, we feel bored.

3. Boredom can lead to a false sense of inspiration. Here's how it usually works: You feel bored. You don't like feeling bored. You want to do something different to escape feeling bored. An idea (inspiration) comes to you. You attribute the idea to God, and you're off starting a new program, sermon series, small group, or any other innovative idea.

Because we are susceptible to mistaking escapes from boredom for inspiration we need to humbly bring our "inspiration" to God in prayer, asking Him to help us recognize whether our eureka moment is from Him, or has its origins in our desire to not be bored.

Let's review.

It's hard to be content in the ministry because:
- we're trying to produce results that are hard to measure.
- there is always someone whose church seems to be doing better.
- there is a constant flow of new ideas, and "the latest thing."
- we're worried that contentment will lead to complacency.
- the driven, type A personality is rewarded in our culture.

- our culture narrowly defines success using three words: *bigger*, *more*, and *new*.
- we can get bored with the routines that make up pastoring.

Remember in the previous chapter we said that energy, equanimity, and contentment are found in the closet?

As with energy and equanimity, our contentment will be in direct proportion to the consistency and meaningfulness of our times alone with God. The closet can change us from discontented to contented...but this takes time. Contentment is seldom achieved in one sitting. In our closet, in that peaceful place, the Father of peace waits for us. Do you struggle with contentment? Go to your closet.

Questions for reflection:

1. On a scale of one to ten (ten being high), how would I score my current contentment in my life and ministry?

2. What one thing could I do to raise my score by one point?

six

Demystifying Mysticism

"Speak Father, I am listening for your voice."
1 Sam. 3:10

There are certain words that make some Protestant pastors nervous. While those in the Orthodox, Anglican, and Catholic streams of Christianity have no problem with these words, those of us who fall under the category of Protestant can get a bit skittish and come up with a bunch of objections any time we hear words like: *monasticism, monk, contemplative, reflective, mystic, mysticism, mystical,* and *meditation.*

Part of our uneasiness can be traced back to the Protestant Reformation that resulted in throwing out just about everything associated with the Roman Catholic Church. For example, since Catholics were big on monks, monasticism, and mysticism, then monks, monasticism, and mysticism became a "Catholic-thing;" and since some thought there was a good chance that the Pope was the Antichrist, Protestants wanted nothing to do with monks, monasticism, or mysticism.

In addition to this, you've got Hindus and Buddhists and New-Agers that meditate, while Jews and Muslims have a history of mysticism. And after all, *mystic* sounds a lot like the word *magic*, which makes us think of Harry Potter...so it's just best if we distance ourselves from the whole crazy thing.

But do words like *monasticism*, *monk*, *contemplative*, *reflective*, *mystic*, *mysticism*, *mystical*, and *meditation* relate only to Catholics and the super, super spiritual? Or, is there a place for them in the lives of all believers, and specifically, in the lives of pastors?

• • •

Demystifying the Mystical

I suggest that we look at our list of words, come up with a simple definition for each one, and then see if we can warm up to them a bit.

Monasticism will be the hardest for us. With **monasticism** we come up with images of monasteries filled with monks wearing robes and spending their days in prayer and meditation while voluntarily saying no to things we couldn't possibly imagine living without. I had one pastor tell me, "I could never be a monk—I like sex too much." Now that's just funny.

We are beginning to see small groups of Protestants joining together in monastic-type communities. And for some time now, Protestant Christians have been visiting Catholic retreat centers to practice spiritual disciplines for anywhere from one day to a full week. I do understand if you have trouble getting your mind around all the words and practices often associated with monasticism and therefore see no place for monasticism in a non-Catholic Christian's walk with God. Let's just make sure we don't throw the monk out with the bathwater. Speaking of the word *monk*...

I don't think I'm tough enough to be a **monk**. I like my belongings too much to take a vow of poverty. I don't trust people, so it would be difficult for me to take a vow of obedience and put much of my life in the hands of another person. I've got too much to say to take a vow of silence. And as far as celibacy...well, need I say more?

I'm not attracted to the word *monk* as a noun. I am far more comfortable with it as a verb. In other words, I don't want to be a monk, I want to embrace the values and practices of a monk as much as I can without taking formal vows and moving into a monastery. I want to monk. (I'll talk more about this later in chapter 8.)

Next we have the words **contemplative** and **reflective**. Sometimes these two words are used as nouns to describe monks or nuns (contemplatives, reflectives), and sometimes they are used as verbs to describe what monks and nuns tend to do a lot of (contemplate, reflect). If I were to ask your typical pastor, "Is there anything wrong with a believer sitting and contemplating or reflecting upon scripture or some other spiritual truth?" The answer would be, "Certainly not."

And now for the triplets: mystic, mysticism, and mystical. Let me suggest a simple three-fold definition of a mystic. A **mystic** is one who believes God can be experienced, has some experience in experiencing God, and helps others experience God for themselves.

Pastor, let me ask you, according to that definition, wouldn't you consider yourself a mystic? I hope you answered yes—though I wouldn't necessarily suggest you add *mystic* to your business card.

Mystics believe God can be experienced, and they base this belief on their understanding of the Bible and their own personal experience. **Mysticism** is the practice of spiritual disciplines—such as, but not limited to, prayer, scripture meditation, solitude, and fasting—all of which help one experience God. **Mystical** is how we describe the actual experience one has with God. For example, when we say, "I felt God say to me…," we are claiming a mystical experience.

That doesn't sound too weird, does it?

Finally, we come to **meditation**. The word *meditation*, or a variation of the word, appears twenty-three times in the Bible. Now that's not a lot of occurrences when you consider how big the Bible is, but it is enough to admit that *meditation* is a biblical word.

Meditation is best understood as simply taking time to think about or focus on spiritual things. One problem some have with meditation is that people of other religions meditate. Just because practitioners of other faiths meditate doesn't mean we can't, nor does it mean that meditation means the same thing to us as it does to them.

Questions for reflection:

1. What words could I substitute for: monasticism, monk, contemplative, reflective, mystic, mysticism, mystical, and meditation?

2. Are there any of these words that make me feel uncomfortable? If so, why?

3. Have I ever had a mystical experience?

4. If there is anything a person could do to foster mystical experiences, what might that be?

seven

"But What About...?"

"Jesus, I don't mean this to sound like an excuse,
but my parents need my help. Would you mind
if I joined your team after they passed away?"
Matt. 8:21

I know, I know, up until chapter 6 you were loving this book, but after all that talk about becoming a mystic you have a string of objections.

Objection #1: Dave, you don't understand, I'm an extrovert. I'm not wired for all this contemplative business.

I do understand. I understand that you are an extrovert, but what's that got to do with contemplation? The first assumption is that only introverts are drawn to solitude, prayer, meditation, and reflection. The second assumption is that being an extrovert is something you're locked into with no hope of venturing beyond those walls.

I suppose that some of the spiritual disciplines might come more easily to an introvert than an extrovert. I'm an introvert. Crowds drain me. Therefore, solitude is absolutely no problem for me.

We recently decided to go from owning two cars to one. Ellen takes our only car to work. This is wonderful because it gives me a reason never to leave my house. Some of my children are worried about me.

"Dad, you've got to get out more."
"Why?"
"Because it's not good for you to be alone all the time."
"Why?"
"Because God created us to be in relationship with others."
"I am in relationship with others. I talk to pastors all day long."
"That's different."
"Why?"
"Because it is. You know I'm right."

They probably are right. My point is that I am an introvert, but that doesn't mean that contemplation is nessesarily easier for me.

Objection #2: I've tried to be more spiritual but failed—and failed, and failed again.

Me, too. I understand what that's like. Keep trying anyway. Besides, what do you mean by *tried* and what do you mean by *failed?* Sometimes our problem is not having tried and failed, but having tried the wrong way in the first place. One size does not fit all.

Keep trying and experimenting until you discover practices and a routine that work for you. I'll talk more about this later in my last chapter, "Baby Steps."

Objection #3: It's too hard.

I agree: it is hard. It's not complicated, but it is hard.

Trying to become a pastor-mystic is hard, but so is not becoming a pastor-mystic. It's hard to always feel spiritually dry. It's hard to feel you never have any mystical experiences of your own to share. It's hard to feel like God is a distant cousin you see maybe once a year instead of a Father who loves you and wants to keep company with you. It's hard to feel like the ministry is sucking the life out of you. It's hard to lose your joy, your motivation, and your energy. It's hard to always be talking about the spiritual life you wish you had.

Developing a more meaningful (mystical) and consistent devotional life is something we both long for and run from at the same time. It's hard, but it's only hard. Hard is not the same as impossible. Have you ever achieved anything worthwhile in life that was not hard? They call them spiritual disciplines because they take discipline, because they are hard…at first.

Yes, it's hard, but embrace the hard.

Objection #4: I'm too busy.

Well that's probably true. I have learned from my experience in working with pastors (and having been one myself) that most pastors are too busy. But let me ask you this. If you don't have time to spend in solitude with God, do you have time to feel spiritually dry?

Do you have time to:
- feel you never have any mystical experiences of your own to share?
- feel your walk with God is more like a relationship with a distant cousin you see maybe once a year rather than a present Father who loves you and wants to keep company with you?
- feel like the ministry is sucking the life out of you?
- lose your joy, your motivation, and your energy?
- always be talking about the spiritual life you wish you had?

Wait…didn't I just say something like that?

You can't make time for God. You can only "take" time for God. Ministry is like playing tug-of-war. You're at one end of the rope and the church, or your schedule, is on the other end. If you're not stronger than your opponent, your calendar will fill up instead of your soul.

Objection #5: The mystics that I've read about are way out of my league. I could never be like them.

You're probably right. Most of them were off the charts when it came to commitment to God and the pursuit of spirituality. Some of them even seemed a bit crazy at times. But remember, just because someone is crazy doesn't mean what they experience is not real. Do you remember comedian Lilly Tomlin? She once said, "Why is it that when we talk to God we call it prayer, but when we say God talked to us we call it crazy?"

The good news is: you don't have to be a hermit or an anchorite (I'll let you look that one up) in order to become closer to God. The Father doesn't expect you to quit your job and take monastic vows. You'll never be Francis of Assisi, Teresa of Avila, Brother Lawrence, Julian of Norwich, or John of the Cross. All of these people were extreme examples of what it looks like to pursue intimacy with God.

More recent mystics and writers on mysticism, such as Thomas Merton and Evelyn Underhill, along with the "oldies" listed above should not become objects of imitation but of inspiration. They are guides on the same road we are on. Granted, they are way out ahead of us and probably always will be. We see them like a small dot on the horizon. If we listen carefully enough we can hear them calling, "This way, this way. Don't worry about catching up, just keep coming this way."

Leave the objections and start moving toward that dot on the horizon.

Questions for reflection:

1. Which of the five objections can I relate to the most?

2. Imagine someone comes to me with the objection I just chose. How would I invalidate it?

3. Do I have an objection not on Dave's list? What is it? If someone came to me with that objection how would I shoot holes in it?

eight

To Monk

Develop spiritual routines that will ensure you become the type of person God wants you to be.
1 Tim. 4:7b

As a noun, the word *monk* represents a discipline of life unattainable and undesirable for most of us. It's doubtful that many of us are going to cloister ourselves away in a monastery, taking on a vow of poverty, chastity, and obedience. We love our possessions, sex, and independence too much. Like a pair of pants one size too small, monk as a noun just doesn't fit us very comfortably.

If we're Protestants we struggle with monks theologically. Our thoughts may run something like this: monks believe in purgatory, give homage to Mary, pray to the saints, and teach something called transubstantiation. If we've done any kind of study into early church history, we most certainly have run across stories of monks, and their even more radical friends, the hermits. Who wants to starve themselves to near-death, live in the desert, sleep on the ground, and go without any of the comforts we've grown accustomed to? (All of which, I might add, is an unfair caricature of most hermits.) To use monk as a noun, to be a monk, seems unnecessary if not unfortunate. When we see a monk on the street or in a movie, we might feel sorry for them. (The funny thing is, they often feel sorry for us.) Look at all they're missing. But are they the ones missing out, or could we be the ones?

As I see it, the word *monk* must change from a noun to a verb or we will never learn to benefit from this ancient form of Christianity. We don't have to believe everything a monk believes in order "to monk." We can remain a Baptist, a Pentecostal, or a Lutheran, and still monk. And might I suggest that not only can we monk—but monk, we must. Why do I say such a thing?

"Superficiality is the curse of our age. The doctrine of instant satisfaction is a primary spiritual problem. The desperate need today is not for a greater number of intelligent people, or gifted people, but for deep people."[17]

Those who monk become deeper people. The spiritually shallow will never adorn the gospel enough to make it something attractive to those who need it.

Let's face it. When people outside the church look at those of us inside the church, they often don't see much of a difference. Our divorce rate is about the same, we struggle with the same addictions, and we can be just as prejudiced, self-righteous, unforgiving, and mean as the next person. Our "religion" has had little effect on our materialism, our consumerism, our fascination with celebrities, and all that we call entertainment. We are just as busy, stressed, and worried as those who make no profession of faith. Our children can be just as ill behaved, despite a steady exposure to a great children's ministry at our church. We drive as fast, eat as much, and find humor in the same things everyone else does. When we invite those outside to join us, what are we asking them to join? We've already joined them! It's hard to admit, but we're not really all that different from those who don't profess faith in Christ.

We've been brainwashed, bamboozled, tricked. Our culture, particularly if we live in a western society, has slowly infected us, and we are barely aware of it. In fact, pretty much all of the things we've had contact with from birth up to the present—our parents, our schools, our friends, mass-media, and sometimes even the church—have all played a part in making us less than who we were created to be. We are not whole. We are partial at best.

My true self—that part of me made in the image of God—has been suppressed, pushed down, and buried. That which is on the surface, what is seen by those around me, is my false self. In *Seeds*, an excellent compilation of the different themes found in the writings of Thomas Merton, editor Robert Inchausti says, "The world cultivates the false self, ignores the real one, and therein lies the great irony of human existence: The more we make of ourselves, the less we actually exist."[18]

If we are ever going to resurrect our true self we must monk.

Questions for reflection:

1. Even if I have a limited understanding of the life of a monk, what aspects of their lives intrigue me?

2. What part of them is transferrable to a non-monk like me?

3. Can I identify any aspects of my true self that have been suppressed? If so, by whom, when, and to what end?

nine

Resistance:

When the Enemy Is You

I don't know what's wrong with me.
I don't practice the things I want to
practice, but instead, I practice the
things I don't want to practice.
Rom. 7:15

In my coaching practice I am often surprised to see some pastors actually avoid talking about their quiet times, or lack of quiet times, with God. Once I venture into this subject, the conversation often shifts from their soul to their church.

"So, Bob, tell me about your prayer life."

"Could be better, but things are going really well at the church. Attendance is up a little."

"I'm glad to hear that, but it sounds like your devotional life could use some improvement?"

"Well, it could always be better. I'll tell you what really could use some improvement is our giving. Could we talk about developing a stewardship program?"

"Sure, Bob."

. . .

Pastors, and the rest of us for that matter, want to be spiritual and yet resist being spiritual at the same time. Henri Nouwen says, "My resistance to solitude has proved as strong as my desire for it."[19]

We wish we were something we are not yet, but we resist the steps necessary to become who we wish we were.

I have found that most pastors don't have a consistent and meaningful devotional life, and many have quit trying to have one. You might think I'm exaggerating but I'm not. Here are some theories I have as to why this is so.

First, it's hard to develop a devotional life, especially if we don't have much of one in the first place or if we have tried and failed repeatedly. In my final chapter, "Baby Steps," I'll share my own story of years of trying and failing, and trying and failing some more, to establish a consistent and meaningful devotional life. It's no wonder things like prayer, meditation, silence, and solitude are called spiritual disciplines. It takes discipline to engage in these practices and discipline is hard—and we tend to resist what is hard and favor what is easy.

Second, we're afraid of what we might hear in the silence. There can actually be some anxiety surrounding the thought of being alone with God. Nouwen put it this way:

> We seem to have a fear of empty spaces. The philosopher Spinoza called this a *horror vacui*. We want to fill up what is empty. Our lives stay very full. And when we are not blinded by busyness, we fill our inner space with guilt about things of the past or worries about things to come. Perhaps part of our fear comes from the fact that an empty place means that something may happen to us that we cannot predict, that is new, that invites leads us to a place we might not want to go. I might not want to hear what God has to say.[20]

For two years I met with a spiritual director, named Russ Ikeda, while transitioning from the pastorate to coaching. Russ gave me a helpful definition of the word *intimacy*: "Intimacy means 'into-me-see.'" Isn't that great?

When I sit quietly with God I am inviting Him to look into me and to share with me what He sees. Silence and solitude with God might make us uncomfortable at first, like looking into the mirror first thing in the morning before we've had a chance to tidy up a bit. If we persist, eventually our times of quiet with God will become the most peaceful and safe place we've ever experienced. Until we experience this, however, the *horror vacui* causes us to resist.

Third, our constant "spiritual activities" can fool us into believing we are more spiritual than we really are. Many pastors give more of themselves to their church or ministry than they do to God. If I confuse my ministerial duties with time spent alone with God, I can draw just enough spiritual nutrients from my job to make it through another day but not enough to sustain a life infused with the power and presence of Jesus.

Fourth, we're just too busy. In *Five Smooth Stones for Pastoral Work*, Eugene Peterson tells us that "busyness is an illness of spirit, a rush from one thing to another because there is no ballast of vocational integrity and no confidence in the primacy of grace."[21]

The busier our lives are, the harder it will be for us to take the time to sit quietly with God. When we do force ourselves to sit down we will be reminded of all the important things to be done today. Then the temptation is to give in to the distractions, cut our time short, and go on about our day.

Finally, in any discussion as to why we find it so difficult to cultivate our inner life, we must not forget the devil.

Certainly our adversary is content to find us any place other than in our prayer closet. The devil couldn't care less about our ministry activities as long as our souls are shallow and Jesus seems like a distant cousin rather than our Savior-friend. The reproduction of intimacy with Jesus in the lives of those we minister to flows out of our own intimacy with Jesus. Our true identity, the beloved of God, takes root and grows as we spend time with our Father. If our enemy can keep us from that place then he will succeed, and we will only be able to reproduce a superficial spirituality in the people we've been called to pastor.

Thomas Merton said, "Those who cannot be alone cannot find their true being and they are less than themselves."[22] Haven't you felt that there must be more to life than you are experiencing? Pay attention—that longing for more is your true being crying out for Jesus.

The restlessness and resistance we feel toward solitude with God is an indication of something we need to face and overcome. We need to be courageous enough to sit still and invite God to "into-me-see." He will come. He will see. He will share with us what He has found. He will be gentle. He will help us overcome the resistance. Once we overcome the resistance, we will be overcome by Him.

Questions for reflection:

1. Of the five reasons why we resist spending time alone with God, which one can I relate to the most?

2. What steps could I take to overcome this resistance?

ten

Sermon Fodder or Soul Food?

When I read your word my
weak heart is energized.
Ps. 119:50

I wonder what effect it would have on our sermons if we spent as much time meditating on the scriptures for personal edification as we do studying the scriptures for sermon preparation? In other words, let's say you meditate on the scriptures two hours a week for your own spiritual formation and study the scriptures six hours a week for your Sunday message. What would happen if you reversed that? Would your sermon be better, worse, or the same?

Don't get me wrong. Ask anyone who has used me as a preaching coach and they will tell you how much I value sermon preparation. I believe that study can be a very spiritual experience. However, we must remind ourselves that the Bible wasn't primarily given to us for our sermons but for our souls.

So which is best—studying the scriptures or meditating on the scriptures? It doesn't have to be either/or. It can be both/and. The problem is...seldom is it both/and.

Many of the pastors I talk to admit that the only time they are consistently in the Bible is when they are preparing their sermons. This is not entirely without benefit as far as soul-care is concerned. Any time the word of God goes into our minds we profit, but when we study we tend to have our preacher-hat on.

When I have my preacher-hat on I approach my Bible to dissect it, tear it apart, exegete it. Commentaries, Greek and Hebrew aids, Bible dictionaries, and concordances surround me. I'm looking for the original intent of the author. I'm asking myself, "How might this passage preach?" With my preacher-hat on, I tend to read and study the Bible academically.

As pastors, most of us are good at this. We've been trained in hermeneutics and homiletics. We might even have degrees in Bible and theology. We've spent thousands of dollars on the books we've accumulated over the years that line our walls. An academic approach to the Bible can result in a solid sermon. However, there is no guarantee that it will be the method by which our relationship with Jesus is impassioned, our heart softened, our self-will broken, our eyes opened, or our life deepened.

I'm not suggesting we throw out our preacher-hat; it serves a very legitimate purpose. What we really need is to add to our hat collection one that will help us experience something different than the preacher-hat we typically wear when we come to the Bible. Might I suggest that we need a monk-hat as well?

Although monasticism has produced its fair share of scholars and theologians, monks typically approach the Bible as the very life and breath of God. The book of Hebrews tells us that the word of God is "living and active." Those in monastic orders relate to scripture as the living thing it claims to be.

It is not unusual for monks to be called con-templatives or reflectives. When I open my Bible wearing my monk-hat, I read it in a contemplative, reflective way. My goal is not so much to gain infor-mation, as it is to gain spiritual formation. I am chewing on the words slowly, rolling them around in my mouth like a bite of truffle, and tasting the goodness of God for me the child of God...not for me the sermon-crafter.

• • •

A while back I wrote an article for my blog entitled "God in My Hands," which was originally a journal entry of mine. I was a bit nervous putting it out there because I knew there might be some who felt I was deifying the

Bible. That is not my intention or position, so please bear that in mind while you read.

Journal entry from March 16, 2012:
> Ps. 1:2-3
>
> The Bible delights me. I love it. I delight in the Lord. I love the Lord. I realize that the Bible is not God, but if it is the word of God, is it not, in a sense, God? Can we separate God from His word? I know that the book I hold in my hands is not God in my hands, not literally, but what harm does it do to think, "This is His word, this is God. I am holding Him, listening to Him, praying, and meditating upon Him...here, in my hands?"
>
> We have the ability to hold God. Holding God. I realize this will bring objections by many, and rightly so, I understand.
>
> We don't want to say the Bible is God, but it's close enough, and I think we should be able to relax and not miss my point.
>
> I have no problem whatsoever thinking that when I sit down with my Bible I am sitting down with God, or when I feel the Bible speaking to me that God is speaking to me. I am comfortable, quite comfortable saying, "This morning God told me..." and what I am referring to is a passage of Scripture I have read. Very comfortable indeed.
>
> I delight in the Bible. I meditate on the Bible. The Bible causes me to prosper. I delight in God. I

meditate on God. God causes me to prosper. I'm quite comfortable with this way of thinking.

• • •

There is a time to put on the preacher-hat, and there is a time to put on the monk-hat. One will result in a solid sermon and the other, a solid spirituality. Which do you want more? Which do you need more? The good news is that you can have both. It's only a problem if you don't wear both hats.

If meditating upon the scriptures is new to you, let me introduce to you Benedict of Nursia (AD 480-547) and the practice of Lectio Divina. This will be a good starting point for getting your monk-hat on.

The Latin term *Lectio Divina*, which means *spiritual or divine reading*, is the ancient practice of meditating upon the word of God, taught and popularized by Saint Benedict, founder of the Benedictines. Recently, Lectio Divina has been gaining popularity among Protestants. There are many variations of Lectio, some more complicated than others. The following is how I coach those who are interested in this practice.

First of all, find a Bible that has paragraph headings.

I recommend beginning the practice of Lectio with one of the Gospels.

Select half a chapter, a parable, one single story or narrative, or simply use the chapter headings to determine what passage you will focus on.

Find a quiet place that is free of distraction and get comfortable.

It's really important to read your selection slowly and straight through. After the first reading, sit silently for at least a minute. Then read the same passage again, slowly. Repeat the minute of silence.

You are listening and looking for something that stands out to you. It might be a word or phrase. Sometimes your imagination will take you into the story itself as you picture what it would have been like to be there. Read the passage one more time, slowly, followed by your final minute of silence.

You will read the passage through a total of three times, each time followed by silence. Don't try to make something happen. It's possible that all you will experience is a time of scripture reading followed by silence. This is okay. It is very likely that after you get used to this practice, you will experience many ways in which the Father will speak to you.

After you've read through your passage, take the things that caught your attention (words, images, thoughts) and use them as your starting point for journaling and prayer. I'll discuss journaling in more depth in chapter 12.

I have found it meaningful to begin with Lectio Divina. I then let the scriptures lead me to the focus for my journaling. Finally, I let what I've journaled lead me to my focus for prayer.

This is my way of connecting with God. It's not the only way to connect with God. You have to discover your way to connect with God. But this way is a good way to begin.

If you are new to Lectio it might take a little time for you to get the hang of it. Many people, when starting out, report there is a slight learning curve. This is normal and to be expected.

Once you grow comfortable with reading the scriptures this way, once you become more reflective and contemplative in your use of the Bible, once you put your monk-hat on, you will experience a whole new relationship with the Word of God and the God of His Word. Get your monk-hat on.

Questions for reflection:

1. If I already practice Lectio Divina what is it that I find most helpful or enjoyable?

2. If I already practice Lectio Divina, in what ways does my practice differ from the one Dave described?

3. If I don't practice Lectio Divina what is it about this discipline that I find the most intimidating or challenging?

eleven

The Love of Sleep

Stop being so infatuated with sleep.
Prov. 20:13

I can still remember as if it happened last week: It was the middle of the night and I was walking one of our babies. (Ellen did the nursing; I did the walking. We tried it the other way around but it didn't quite work the same.) I'd been doing this for a few nights in a row, and I was tired. My days were feeling the effect of sleep deprivation. During the day this little girl was the most beautiful thing I'd ever laid my eyes on—perfect, sweet, and adorable. But on this night, as I looked down into her wide-open eyes, I saw her for what she really was. That little bundle was trying to kill me. She didn't care how I felt, or how exhausted I was. She didn't appreciate the previous nights when I shuffled through the dark recesses of our home like a zombie. I remember thinking, "This is going to kill me. I can't go on like this. If I don't get more sleep I'm going to die."

The next morning I confessed my feelings to Ellen. Certainly she would understand how important it was for me to get a good night's sleep. After all, I needed to be at my best to serve the spiritual needs of the people I'd been called to pastor. She listened patiently, looked at me with love in her eyes, and said, "It's only tired. It won't kill you." There was a dramatic pause. She stared at me; I stared at her. I blinked, she didn't. It was over, and I lost. But that night, when I was up again walking the baby, I had time to think about her words and reluctantly I agreed: It's only tired. It won't kill me.

• • •

Someone once said that the greatest obstacle to the spiritual life is a love of sleep. I might add to that a fear of being tired. We love sleep, and we fear feeling tired.

Here's the thing. In regards to spending time alone with God, any time other than first thing in the morning is risky. First thing is the only sure thing. I'm not saying that having a quiet time in the middle of the day or evening will not work. Times like this can be just as meaningful but they are twice as likely (maybe more so) to be interrupted or postponed. And what does this have to do with a love of sleep and a fear of feeling tired?

For most of us, if we are going to start our day with time alone with God, if we don't want to be interrupted by the family or by morning appointments, we will have to get up earlier than we would like to. We will have to, oh forgive me for saying this, set our alarm clock earlier. A good alarm clock is the best devotional tool you will ever have.

Now, I can already hear the objections: "I'm not a morning person. If I get up earlier I'll feel tired. It's better for me to meet with God later in the day." Okay, let's look at these arguments one by one.

Objection #1: I'm not a morning person.

This could be true. Some people can pop out of bed with a smile on their face, a clear head, and a song on their lips. Others hold on to their pillows like a man clutching a life preserver after having been swept overboard. For some waking up is easy, for others it's hard. But honestly, haven't there been times in your life when you had to set your alarm clock either for work or something else? When you did, when you got up early, did it kill you?

I thought about drawing your attention to Mark 1:35 ("When it was early in the morning, before the sun came up, Jesus left the house and went off to a quiet and remote place where he prayed.") but making a principle out of a single verse is poor hermeneutics, not to mention an attempt to motivate by guilt and shame, and even though we pastors are good at that, I will not go there.

So, while it's true that you might not be a "morning person," consider what is more important to you: to stay in bed and stay the way you are, or set your alarm a bit earlier to insure that you have time to cultivate intimacy with God?

Objection #2: If I get up earlier I'll feel tired.

Yes, you probably will. But is feeling tired really that horrible? Think about it. Feeling tired isn't pleasurable but it's not like getting a stick in your eye. Now I realize if you are a bi-vocational pastor who has a day job as a brain surgeon, then maybe you don't want to poke around gray matter if you're tired and struggling to keep your eyes open. But other than that...you'll be okay. Your body will adjust.

Maybe you need to go to bed earlier or plan for a short nap in the middle of your day. The bottom line is this: would you rather feel physically tired or spiritually empty?

Objection #3: It's better for me to meet with God later in the day.

I hear this a lot. I usually respond by asking, "So how's that working for you?" The typical answer is, "Well...not as well as I would like. Often something else interrupts me." Exactly.

If you are able to maintain a meaningful, consistent quiet time with God in the middle of your day, one that is peaceful and unrushed, then more power to you. Keep it up. But if not, take this challenge.

Compare early morning quiet times with middle of the day quiet times. Set a goal of three to four days a week. Take one month and experiment with early morning quiet times and one month with middle of the day quiet times. At the end of the two months ask yourself which approach proved to be more consistent and meaningful. Do what works best for you. Just remember, your current devotional routine is perfectly designed to give you the results you are getting. If you want different results you will probably have to do something different.

There is a good chance that what you need to do is just set that stupid alarm clock and when it goes off, pop immediately out of bed. If your problem is falling back asleep after turning the alarm off, then place your alarm far enough away from your bed that you are forced to get out of bed to turn it off. Just do it. Don't let a love of sleep and a fear of being tired keep you from a deeper relationship with God.

Questions for reflection:

1. Of the three objections given above, which one can I relate to the most?

2. What steps would I have to take to overcome that objection?

3. Do I have an objection not listed above?

4. What would I have to do to overcome that objection?

twelve

Spiritual Journaling

I will reflect, over and over, on all You are
doing in my life, and consider what You
are trying to say and do in my life.
Ps. 77:12

My Journal on Journaling

I've often thought my best writing is in my journals. Since this chapter is on the subject of journaling I thought I'd begin by letting my journal speak on journaling.

January 4, 2007:

> Journaling answers the questions, "What's going on inside of me, or what's happening around me and how am I interacting with it?" Journaling is a pausing in your day to reflect, to be self-aware. There is a shallowness of soul that settles in without reflection. Journaling records reflection. The Spirit uses

reflection to bring to our attention the things hidden below the surface. There is much hidden.

One always has a need for self-awareness. The need for reflection, to be a Reflective, never goes away. There are many enemies of reflection. We must rebel against them by scheduling time to be self-aware, to journal.

February 24, 2007:

Journaling records what's going on inside of me, outside of me, surrounding me. What am I thinking? How am I responding? This discipline provides a space for the Spirit to invade, mixing His thoughts with mine and producing a hybrid of self-awareness and insight. In journaling, the flesh joins hands with the Spirit to lead the soul further on the journey.

May 29, 2007:

I record my thoughts, what I see and hear, what I'm feeling. Such investigation cuts through the façade and reaches the true self. The important stuff is usually buried so deep one would never know it was there. Like a vein of gold or an underground artesian well. Beauty, life...but hidden, unknown, unappreciated. Useless.

That which is hidden, neglected, can only expect to deteriorate, rust, decompose. Actually a mutation occurs. The hidden, true self atrophies and becomes replaced by the false self until that which is false is believed to be that which is true. The real true becomes forgotten, almost impossible to resurrect. Journaling is an attempt to bring to life the true. Prayer, meditation, silence and solitude, journaling, are rain upon the hard soil of our souls.

August 10, 2007:

Often my journaling is like taking a road I've never been down before. A trail leading me I know not where. I just start writing and words, thoughts, feelings begin to pour out from pen to page. There is an adventure in it...this exploration of self.

It is, of course, more comfortable to know where you are going, but you always owe your knowing to someone who went before you...someone willing to blaze the trail. And so, I have an obligation to set out and see where I end up. I walk on a path left by others and I leave my own path as well. It is the adventurous, the inquisitive, the explorers that leave something behind. So...what shall I write about today?

September 30, 2008:

With journaling it can sometimes seem like the pen has a life of its own. I can have no direction and yet the pen will take me someplace...from nowhere to somewhere. Other times I intend to write one thing and end up in an entirely different place. The pen takes over. The end result is usually deep. Either way, there is an anticipation as one sits down to journal because you never know what is going to come out, where the pen will lead.

• • •

Journaling is a form of meditation. You can count on journaling and meditation to bring you somewhere.

Getting Started with Journaling

I believe journaling is something you become better at over time. Maybe better isn't the right word. Perhaps "more comfortable with" is more accurate.

If you're not much of a reflective type, or you don't enjoy writing, you might feel a bit awkward at first and find yourself staring at a blank piece of paper, waiting for inspiration to crash through the roof. I promise you, it won't. I can assure you, however, that if you stick with it, over time you will develop a friendship with your journal and welcome with anticipation each opportunity to sit, think, write, and pray, which is to say—to journal.

If journaling is new to you I recommend the following process.

Go out and buy a notebook, or better yet, a hardbound blank book. Most office supply stores carry these. I favor handwriting over typing. There are a couple of reasons for this. First, I type fast and the slowness required for handwriting is more conducive to relaxed reflection. Second, there are too many potential distractions that can pop up on your screen and sabotage the moment if you are keeping a journal on your computer.

BING! "Hey Dave, check out a video of this guy falling off a roof. It's hilarious!"

Next, find a quiet place to journal. In journaling, focus is essential; therefore you want to minimize distractions. The one exception to this is the distraction of nature, which is not really a distraction at all, but a wonderful and helpful environment for journaling. Some of my most meaningful times of writing have been when I was outdoors.

It's helpful to be as physically comfortable as possible. I have my big, cushy, God-chair. I call it my God-chair not because God sits in it but because I do when meeting with God. I sit next to a window that looks out over fields, forest, and mountains. The bottom line? Find a place that will be comfortable and quiet.

Finally, get your Bible. Scripture reading is the best launching pad for journaling. Eventually you will be able to journal in a meaningful way without relying on your Bible but most of my journaling gets its start after meditating on the scriptures.

Choose a small portion of a chapter. The Gospels are great for this if journaling is new to you. Read the portion slowly two or three times. (Remember chapter 10's description of Lectio Divina?) As you do this, certain words or phrases will stand out to you. If you are reading a narrative you may find yourself imagining what it would be like to be inserted into the story. Questions might pop into your mind and center around words like: *what, why, who, how?*

I can guarantee that something will rise to the surface and get your attention. When that happens, begin to write about it. Let your thoughts, feelings, and insights flow out of your pen. Remember, no one is going to grade this. In fact, no one is going to read this.

Don't concern yourself with length. Don't worry about grammar. Don't be bothered if you think you sound too spiritual or too stupid. After all, aren't we all a mixture of spiritual and stupid?

When you feel you're done, ask yourself if there is anything you've written that you could pray about. If there is...pray about it.

Questions for reflection:

1. If I am already practicing journaling what is it that I find most helpful or enjoyable?

2. If I don't practice journaling what is it about journaling that I find the most intimidating or challenging?

3. In what ways is journaling a form of meditation?

thirteen

Uncomfortable Reading

*God inspires wise men to write their words
down so that later on He can use their writings to motivate us and nail us down to spiritual
truth. Build a library with books such as these.*

Eccles. 12:11

Fred Smith Sr. has been a mentor to some of the most
well-known Christian leaders of our day. Fred popularized the phrase, "Leaders are readers," and also said,
"Make clear decisions about what you read and why."[23]

Most pastors are readers, but they read too much of
the same thing. By this I mean that pastors tend to grav-
itate toward books dealing with the ministry—reading
for information rather than spiritual formation. I often
wish they would read books other than the ones they
take the time to read.

It is always somewhat exciting to start a new book—
especially one you have reason to believe will be really

good. Clean, stiff, untouched...soon it will be bent, written on, underlined, stained. I'm not nice to my books. And a good book will not be nice to me.

There is a place, I guess, for nice books, but the best books are never nice. Good books are intrusive, forceful, and inconsiderate of your feelings and comfort. A good book, unlike a nice book, confronts, challenges thought, and forces you to think, reconsider, or change. A good book will take you where you've never been before—often times kicking and screaming.

Most pastors read, but they read nice books. It's a shame that with the little amount of time they do have to read that they bother to read the stuff they do: commentaries, church growth/management, books that develop their skills or give them new ways of doing the same old thing, all the while ignoring the books that deal with the pastor's true self—his center or her soul.

Balanced people are balanced readers. There are three types of reading: educational, recreational, and inspirational.

1. Educational: For pastors this means books like commentaries, leadership development, church health/growth, etc.
2. Recreational: Fun stuff, reading just for the pleasure of it. Nothing work related.
3. Inspirational: Reading that stretches your soul. With this type of reading, you are not looking for information

as much as inspiration—inspiration that deepens your intimacy (into-me-see) with Jesus.

All three are needed for balance. Most pastors are good at educational and recreational reading, but not so good at inspirational reading. What are you reading for inspiration?

I've never been able to confirm this quotation from Thomas à Kempis, so don't quote me on it, but supposedly only one scrap of paper with his actual writing has survived and it reads: "For rest, respite, repose on this earth, I've looked high and low, but couldn't find it, except perhaps in out-of-the-way nooks with out-of-the-ordinary books."

The best books are out of the ordinary, they get your attention and transform your soul, and they form you more than inform you.

• • •

In my office next to my God-chair is my stack of quiet time tools. I have a Bible, a notebook for journaling, and a notebook for writing my prayers. I have a small pad of paper to write things down that I don't want to forget, things that might pop into my mind and distract me. In addition to these, I always have a book I am reading devotionally for spiritual formation. Some of these books are considered spiritual classics, and some of them have been written by contemporary authors who focus on the inner life. Francis Bacon wrote, "Some books are to be tasted, others are to be swallowed, and some few to be chewed and digested."[24]

Over the years there have been many books that I have chewed and digested for the purpose of spiritual formation. Here are some examples:

- *A Monk's Alphabet* by Jeremy Driscoll
- *The Seeking Heart* by François Fénelon
- *The Practice of the Presence of God* by Brother Lawrence
- *Devotional Classics, Selected Readings for Individuals and Groups* edited by Richard Foster and James Bryan Smith
- Any volume from the Rekindling the Inner Fire series edited by David Hazard
- *Shepherds Balm* by Richard Earl
- *The Wisdom of the Desert* arranged by Thomas Merton
- *My Utmost for His Highest* by Oswald Chambers
- *A Simple Path* by Mother Teresa
- *The Essential Wisdom of the Saints* edited by Carol Kelly-Gangi

For the really, really serious reader:

- *Interior Castle* by Saint Teresa of Avila
- *Dark Night of the Soul* by Saint John of the Cross
- *Experiencing the Depths of Jesus Christ* by Jeanne Guyon

My two favorite books on the spiritual disciplines:

- *Celebration of Discipline* by Richard Foster
- *The Life You've Always Wanted* by John Ortberg

• • •

My favorite spiritual writer of all time is Thomas Merton. In all my years of reading, no single writer has had more influence on my spiritual formation than Thomas Merton. Merton said, "For there are people one meets—in books and in life—with whom a deep resonance is at once established"[25] and their books "open up a new road"[26] for you. For some reason, Merton has been one of those people for me. If you are unfamiliar with Merton, the book *Seeds*, edited by Robert Inchausti, is a great introduction to his writings, and is, in itself, a great book to use devotionally. I always recommend *Seeds* to those who want to start reading Merton. When Merton was alive he endorsed *A Thomas Merton Reader* for those interested in getting to know him and his work. Both are excellent introductions.

• • •

Here are some helpful questions to ask to determine if a book is a spiritual classic, or a spiritual-formation-focused book, that can serve the inspirational category of reading:

1. Does this book have anything to do with church growth, church management, pastoral skills, philosophy

of ministry, biblical commentary, Greek or Hebrew word study, or leadership development? If so, it's not what I'm talking about.

2. Does this book have an obvious focus on spiritual formation, spiritual disciplines, personal intimacy with God or going deeper in one's relationship with God? If so, then it probably is what I'm talking about.

3. Is the book trying to make you more knowledge-able or more spiritual? If the focus is more on educa-tion than formation, then it's not what I'm talking about.

4. Is the author still living? If so, then there's a 50/50 chance it's not a spiritual classic.

Questions for reflection:

1. Do I read more for education, recreation, or inspiration?

2. What type of input do I need more of: education, recreation, or inspiration?

3. Which books on the recommended reading list have I read?

4. Which books on the list would I be interested in reading?

5. Which of these could I buy today?

6. What's stopping me from buying it?

fourteen

The Required Chapter on Prayer

*Be careful when you go to meet with God.
Make sure you are listening more than talking. Don't be like stupid people who are hasty
and impulsive in bringing a matter to God.
Never forget that God is in heaven and you
are on earth. Your prayers aren't more effective because they are long, in fact, they
might be more effective if they are short.*

Eccles. 5:1-2

Although this is not the last chapter in the book, it was
the last chapter I wrote. You see, just when I thought I
was finished, it dawned on me that I hadn't said anything specifically about prayer. How can someone write
a book about spiritual formation for pastors and leave
out the subject of prayer?

I guess I just assumed that pastors know they should
pray. Did I really need to quote scriptures to prove this?
If you're a pastor you've probably taught on prayer

more than once. You don't need to be informed or convinced.

Still, I felt a need to include a chapter on prayer and share some things that you might find helpful.

Over the years I've developed a much broader definition of prayer than I used to hold. Like most new Christians in the 1970s, the need for personal prayer was drilled into me. I'm not suggesting this was a bad thing. It was a good thing. I wish there was more drilling like this today. However, the concepts of prayer that I embraced were very limited.

For example, when I started out, I thought of prayer as those times when I sat with my eyes closed and I talked to God. Sometimes my prayers focused on my personal needs, and other times my prayers were "lifting up" the needs of others (I used a lot more Christianese back then). If you were really spiritual you called this intercession. If you got really good at intercession (I'm not sure how this was ever measured), you could be called an intercessor, or better yet—a prayer warrior. Anyway, for me prayer simply meant bringing my needs to God in one-way communication. Notice that I did not say one-way conversation? Communication can be one-way, conversation cannot.

Here's a spiritual formation formula: communication with God + conversation with God + communion with God = keeping company with God = prayer.

Communication is when I talk to God. Conversation is when God and I communicate back and forth. Communion refers to those times when there is a sense of closeness, harmony, and connection between God and me. These times can include, but are not limited to, traditional prayer. Whenever communion occurs and I am keeping company with God—I am praying.

Let me describe what I mean.

There are a number of things I might do when I sit down to meet with God. Sometimes I sit in silence practicing deep breathing. Sometimes I read my Bible or meditate on the scriptures. I journal. I pray for my needs. I might pray out loud or silently, or I might write my prayers down. I read devotional classics. I might concentrate on an object like a cross, or a picture on my wall or the clouds in the sky. I might sing. Other times I might pray for people. I seldom do all of these at one sitting.

My times with God will look different from day to day. Sometimes I don't even pray per se. I've come to regard all of my practices as forms of prayer. I am communicating, conversing, having communion with, and keeping company with God. For me, it's all prayer.

Some time ago, I decided to quit calling my daily time a *prayer time*. I didn't feel this was accurate. A prayer time gives the impression that all I'm doing during that time is talking to God about my needs and the needs of others. Instead, I prefer to call it my quiet time or my time to be with God.

I spend an hour each day, first thing in the morning, with God. I know this is impressive to some. To be honest, it doesn't impress me at all. I would like to devote more time, and sometimes I do, but normally my time lasts an hour.

There are times when I'm helping a pastor develop a spiritual formation plan that he or she will ask me about my practices. When I tell the pastor that I spend an hour each day, he or she assumes I'm saying that I talk for an hour to God.

"Wow, I can't imagine doing that."

"Doing what?"

"Praying for an hour. What do you pray about all that time?"

Once I clarify how I spend my hour the pastor begins to see this is something relatively easy to attain. I'm not just praying. I'm doing any number of things that, for me, amount to prayer. Now let me address the question, "How much time is enough time?"

My answer? I don't know. You tell me.

How much time can you afford to take? How much time will be enough so that you feel relaxed and unhurried? How much time do you feel is needed for you to connect with God?

For me the starting point for having a leisurely time with God is an hour. Can I achieve that leisure in less than an hour? Yes. Can you? I don't know, you tell me. There is no hard and fast rule for this. No one can tell you how much time is necessary. I'll deal with the time issue more in the final chapter of this book, but the issue is not so much time spent, as it is how meaningful that time is.

• • •

When I was a new Christian, I can't remember how or when, I picked up this idea that a prayer time didn't count unless it reached at least twenty minutes. I know that sounds dumb but that's what I thought. If I reached twenty minutes, then I'd had a good quiet time. If I didn't reach twenty minutes, it didn't quite count. Even if it was a meaningful time but it came in under the twenty-minute mark, I felt like a spiritual failure. Then one day I heard pastor/author Charles Swindoll say that sometimes ten minutes of meaningful time with God could be more than adequate.

It was as if I'd been set free. Not that I was free to settle for ten minutes, but freed to focus on how meaningful my prayer times were instead of how long my prayer times lasted.

So let me ask you again.

- How much time can you afford to take?
- How much time will be enough so that you feel relaxed and unhurried?
- How much time do you feel is needed for you to connect with God?

Your answers to these questions will tell you how much time you need to set apart to be with God.

Finally, the longer I walk with God the more convinced I am that the biggest need I have in my life is simply to be with Him. Prayer is being with Him. He probably wants us to be devoted to prayer because He wants to be with us. If, when we pray, we lose sight of this, we lose sight of prayer, and it becomes less than what the Father wants prayer to be.

The supreme purpose of prayer is to keep company with God. And if this is true, then anything I do to keep company with God becomes prayer...anything.

Questions for reflection:

1. As I look back at the paragraph where Dave describes the various things he does during his quiet times, which ones haven't I tried? Of those I haven't tried, which ones would I like to try?

2. How much time would I need to take in order to spend an unhurried, leisurely time with God?

3. What would have to happen in order for me to take that time?

4. How would my life and ministry be different if I enjoyed a consistent and meaningful time with God?

fifteen

They Need a Mystic

*I have no idea how, but I know a man who
was caught up to the third heaven.*
2 Cor. 12:2

Since it was all the way back in chapter 6, let me share again my simple definitions of the words *mystic, mysticism,* and *mystical*:

- Mystics believe God can be experienced. Mystics base this belief on their understanding of the Bible and their own personal experience.
- Mysticism is the practice of spiritual disciplines—such as, but not limited to, prayer, scripture meditation, solitude, fasting—that help one experience God.
- Mystical is the actual experience one has with God. When we say, "I felt God say to me…," we are claiming to have had a mystical experience.

Having said that, let me say this:

The greatest need today is not for better sermons, better outreach strategies, better mission statements, better and clearer values, better leadership skills, better staff, better volunteers, better small groups, better offerings, or better vision. We don't need more ideas, more opportunities, more systems, or more resources. We have enough books, conferences, and experts willing to tell us what we should do.

The greatest need today is for pastors who know God deeply and experience God regularly. We need mystics in the pulpits, spiritual directors who, from their own depth of soul, know how to take their people by the hand and lead them into experiencing God for themselves. Since spirituality is more caught than taught, we need pastors who have become infected with a virus, not life-threatening but life-giving, a virus passed on by close proximity, a virus called *intimacy (into-me-see) with God.* We need contagious pastors who infect others, not because of what they know but because of who they are.

Mystic shouldn't be added to Paul's list of leadership gifts in Ephesians 4:11-12, it should be assumed. Shouldn't an apostle experience God? Shouldn't a prophet experience God? Shouldn't an evangelist experience God? Shouldn't a pastor-teacher experience God? If we answer yes, then isn't it fair to say that all four of the leader types (or five if you don't believe in hyphens) in Paul's list are mystics?

In her book *Christian Mystics*, Ursula King says, "Thus there is a need for a new mysticism in a new world. Creative mystics are needed to adapt the heritage of the past to the needs of a new season. In the past, the wisdom and insight of mystical knowledge has been handed down within the Christian Church and was tied to its doctrines. But today the situation is much more experimental and open-ended. There remains the question, then, how mystical teachings and practices are best disseminated and transmitted."[27]

May I suggest: one of the best ways for mystical teachings and practices to be disseminated and transmitted is through the encouragement and example of a pastor who has the heart of a mystic.

• • •

Think back for a moment to those Christians from your past that had the greatest impact on you. There was something different about them, wasn't there? They seemed to be more spiritual, or closer to God than others you knew. Just being around them made you feel nearer to God. And even if their maturity or spirituality seemed beyond your grasp, there was something about them that urged you along, making your heart wish for and believe that a closer relationship with Jesus was possible.

Remember our definition of a mystic? A mystic is one who believes that God can be experienced, has some experience in experiencing God, and is good at helping others grow in their experience of God. Don't miss that last phrase, "helping others grow in their experience of God." If this is not the job of a pastor then I don't know what is. If there is anything our people need more from us than this, I don't know what that could be. And if I'm correct, then the really exciting thing is that this is possible for every pastor regardless of his or her education level, church size, or Myers-Briggs score.

You may or may not have a ministry degree. You may or may not have a large church. You may or may not have written a book. You may or may not have been the one asked to speak at a church conference. The name of your church may or may not have appeared on a Top 100 list in some ministry magazine. It doesn't matter if you are an introvert or an extrovert, a great speaker or just adequate, bi-vocational or full-time, tall, short, fat, thin, attractive, or look like the rest of us. If I'm right, then you can be a mystic. If I'm right, then the people who sit in your church staring back at you each week need you to be a mystic.

Questions for reflection:

1. Can I think of someone from my past who, when I was simply near him or her, made me feel nearer to God? Do I know anyone today that makes my heart wish for and believe that a closer relationship with Jesus is possible?

2. How did that person become the type of person they are?

3. How do I imagine my life and ministry would be different if I were more of a mystic?

sixteen

Baby Steps

*Have an intense focus on the development of
your life and ministry. This way everyone will
be able to see the progress you are making.*

1 Tim. 4:5

Baby steps: to make progress on something in small
increments (from the 1991 movie *What About Bob?*).

Bob (Bill Murray): I can't do that. It's too big!
Dr. Leo (Richard Dreyfuss): Baby steps, Bob. Baby
steps.

Back in my college days I remember taking a psychology class that focused on modern psychology theories. I was the only student in the class who was not pursuing a degree in counseling. By then, I'd been a pastor
for about twenty-five years. These students took delight
in tearing into me, and pastors in general, for screwing
up so many people with "pastoral counseling" instead
of pointing them to a professional. They all had some

story about how a pastor had scarred them, or someone they knew, for life. It's hard to argue with someone's experience, so for the most part, I just sat there silently while thinking to myself, "Oh yeah, like no one's ever been screwed up by a professional counselor?"

Anyway, one night the professor showed us a clip from the movie *What About Bob?*, and said Dr. Leo's baby steps concept was an example of behavioral psychology, a theory of psychology founded by John B. Watson that came into vogue after the release of his 1913 paper, "Psychology as the Behaviorist Views It."

To put it simply, Watson believed that anyone's behavior could be changed. Richard Dreyfuss's character, Dr. Leo, believed this could be accomplished by taking baby steps.

Like Bob, you might be thinking, "I can't do what you've been talking about. I can't be a pastor-mystic. I can't be more spiritual."

Like Dr. Leo, I say, "Baby steps, Bob. Baby steps."

• • •

Movement in the right direction, no matter how small, will eventually get you where you want to be. Moving toward a deeper spirituality is not about giant steps but about baby steps. Here's how you can get started.

Step One: Ask God for help.

I've got to believe it warms the Father's heart to hear us cry out to Him:

Father, help me to spend time with You. Motivate me, change me, give me a hunger for solitude with You. I want to know You better and experience You more. My willpower is weak but You are strong. Do for me what I cannot do for myself. Cause me to grow in my intimacy with You and help me with the practices that will take me there.

Step Two: Keep your eye on the real goal.

The goal of prayer, journaling, scripture meditation, silence and solitude, worship, fasting, practicing self-denial is not prayer, journaling, scripture meditation, silence and solitude, worship, fasting, and practicing self-denial. These are simply the ways we draw closer to God, or the practices that help us experience God. The goal is quality time with God. What motivates us is the desire to keep company with the Father, the Son, and the Spirit.

Imagine you are carrying around a toolbox with the words *Spiritual Formation* stenciled on the outside. Inside you find a number of tools you can pull out and use to deepen your soul and draw closer to Jesus. The goal is not the tools. The tools just help you with your project.

Step Three: Expect a fight.

Developing a spiritual life that is meaningful and consistent is hard work. It will not come about without resistance. Sometimes keeping company with God will be effortless. Other times being alone with God will be sabotaged by interruptions, distractions, procrastination, and a strange inner struggle that causes you to avoid the very thing you want.

Step Four: Set specific, realistic, and easily attainable goals.

Don't settle for vague goals. "I'm going to spend more time with God" is too fuzzy. Be more specific. How many days a week do you want to set aside time for God? Which days will work the best for you? Where will you have these meetings? How much time will you spend with God? Specific goals lead to specific results. Unclear goals lead to unclear results.

Be realistic. Don't set the bar too high. In fact, I believe the bar should be so low that you can't help but step over it. It's better to have easily attainable goals and achieve them than to set yourself up for possible defeat with goals that are too ambitious. If you fail you'll feel discouraged and unmotivated.

I think a realistic and attainable goal to begin with would be something like three days a week for fifteen to twenty minutes.

I remember suggesting to one pastor that he start with ten minutes, three days a week. He asked me, "What good could ten minutes do?" I replied, "Right now you're doing nothing. What good is that doing? Going from zero to ten sounds pretty good." We both laughed.

Step Five: Make yourself accountable.

In my coaching practice I am constantly amazed at the power of accountability when trying to bring about personal change.

Not too long ago, about ten minutes into a coaching call, I asked my coachee (that's right, that's what I call them) about an assignment he agreed to during our previous call. I heard laughter.

"What's funny?"
"I was wondering how long it was gonna take you to ask me that. You know one thing I don't like about you?"

More laughter.

"What?" I asked curiously.
"I know you will always hold me accountable to the action steps I set for myself. Sometimes, especially if I didn't do what I said I'd do, I hope that you will forget, but you never do."

More laughter.

"Well, my job is to either move you forward or make you miserable."

Even more laughter.

Find someone to be accountable to. Share your goals with someone. Ask them to check in with you either by phone, text, or e-mail once a week or so. Just knowing that they will be asking you how your progress is going will be enough to trigger your pride (that's right, pride can be used to our advantage) and keep you on track.

Step Six: Be willing to experiment until you find a rhythm and set of practices that work for you.

How you start out might not be the same as how you end up. You might begin with more focus on scripture meditation and a lesser amount of time on journaling; over time, you might reverse that. Silent prayer might work better for you than verbal prayer. I'm really into writing out my prayers. For others this doesn't work. A devotional book might help...or not. Try silence, or worship, or meditation and reflection. If Mondays, Wednesdays, and Fridays no longer work for you, then switch to Tuesdays, Thursdays, and Saturdays.

It might take some time and experimentation for you to discover what works for you, and what results in a meaningful time with God. The first way is not the only way and might not be the best way. Find your way and do it until it doesn't work for you anymore, and then find another way.

Step Seven: When you fall off the horse get back on and leave the guilt behind.

Notice I said *when*, not *if.* There will be days when you won't meet with God as you had planned. Sometimes this will be your fault and sometimes it will be the result of circumstances beyond your control. This has to be expected and accepted. The question is not whether we'll break our spiritual disciplines routine, but what we do after we break them.

I suggest when you fall off the horse that you calmly climb back in the saddle (resuming your practices) and leave guilt on the ground beside your imprint. It does little good to beat yourself up. We get so upset when we fail. It's as if we expected not to.

I'm not surprised when I fail. What surprises me is when I succeed. I'm surprised that I don't fail more, not that I fail as much as I do.

No need to flog yourself. Don't start over; just pick up where you left off.

Step Eight: Watch out for self-righteousness and legalism.

It's unfortunate but few things lend themselves to self-righteousness or legalism quite like pursuing a deeper spirituality. You don't see them at first, but they creep up on you.

Self-righteousness sneaks in suggesting thoughts like, "I've gone 1,463 days without missing a single day of having my quiet time. What day are you on, huh, huh? What's that? You don't have a quiet time? Oh, poor thing. I'll pray for you on day 1,464." We would never actually say this. But do we think it? Sometimes.

Legalism appears in our thoughts saying skewed comments like, "I better not skip my quiet time today. I've got to preach in the morning and I want God to show up." Or, "I bet the reason I had such a bad day was because I didn't have a prayer time." Or, "God is happy with me when I have my devotions but disappointed with me when I don't."

Watch out for the creepers.

Step Nine: Don't let past failures keep you from trying again.

It wasn't until about halfway through my pastoral career that I got serious about soul-care and spiritual formation. Before that, my spiritual life was on and off, hot and cold. I'd hear some sermon or read some book about prayer, feel guilty, make a commitment to prayer, go a few days…and then quit. Some time would go by,

I'd once again hear some sermon or read some book about prayer, feel guilty, make a commitment to prayer, go a few days…and then quit, again.

Does that sound familiar?

I never really struggled with reading my Bible every day, but prayer? That was entirely different. At that time in my spiritual journey, practices like meditation and journaling weren't even on my radar screen. That was about to change.

• • •

In 1997, I attended a pastors' conference in Southern California. One of the main speakers had recently experienced a breakthrough in his own prayer life, which included prayer journaling (the practice of writing out your prayers) and was attempting to inspire his audience—made up mostly of pastors, myself included, more interested in growing their churches than they were in growing their souls—to commit themselves to prayer. I'd heard it all before. He said nothing new. But for some reason it was different this time. Well actually, I know why this time was different.

While listening to the speaker wrap up his message it was as if I saw a hand in front of me motioning for me to come. In my mind I knew this was the Holy Spirit beckoning me to try again. So I said yes. Even though I'd experienced failure after failure, I said yes. I made a commitment to pray (more specifically, to prayer journal) each and every day beginning the next Monday.

The conference ended. I went back to my hotel, and the next day I drove home in time for Sunday morning.

That Sunday was pretty much like any other Sunday. This time, however, after my sermon and before dismissing the crowd, I knew there was something I had to say.

"Before you go, I need to tell you something."

I didn't mean it to sound ominous, but an uncomfortable hush came over the room. The poor people—they probably thought I was going to tell them I was leaving or that I'd fallen into some horrible sin.

"A few days ago at a conference I made a commitment. I committed to pray every day from here on out. I wanted you to know. I want you to hold me accountable. Have a nice week. You are dismissed."

For a couple of seconds there was silence, and then people got up to leave.

Immediately I thought to myself, "You idiot! Why did you tell them? You didn't have to tell them. You could have kept this to yourself, but you told them. Now they're going to check up on you. You know you're gonna fail. And then you'll have to tell them. That was really stupid, Dave."

Monday came. I did it, day one of prayer journaling. Tuesday came, day two. By the time Sunday rolled around I had kept to my commitment for a whole week! Before and after the service people came up to me to ask how I was doing.

"This is day seven."

"Great, Dave, great; you keep that up."

The next Sunday, "So pastor, how's that prayer thing going?"

"This is day fourteen."
"This is day twenty one."
"This is day twenty eight."

Slowly, the inquiries about my spiritual progress began to taper off. People eventually quit asking but I didn't quit counting.

I still can't believe it but I went 1,463 days in a row before skipping a day! But I didn't skip it because I turned my alarm clock off and went back to sleep. I chose to skip it, or, to be more honest, I needed to skip it. Dare I be so bold as to suggest that God told me to skip it?

You see, toward the end of my 1,463-day run, I began to notice some things in me I didn't like. I could recognize a bit of obsession with my growing number. I could tell some pride had entered my heart.

"I'm on day 1,053. How awesome am I?"

I never said that, but I thought it.

I knew that the only way to break the pride in my accomplishment was to skip a day. I knew I had to do it. I felt God was asking me to do it.

It took me a few days to give in, but hey, what do you expect? After all, I'd made it past four years! More than four years of continuous daily prayer! That was something to be proud of which, of course, was the problem. So there was no day 1,464.

I've skipped many days since then but not too many, at least not too many in a row. My norm is still daily quiet times with God but I'm no longer counting, no longer obsessing, and I'm not aware of any pride connected to my spiritual routines.

Every once in a while I'll remember that conference in 1997, the speaker, the following Sunday at church, and the weeks of people asking me, "Hey, Dave, what day are you on?" Mostly I remember the vision of that hand beckoning me to come.

Prayer Journal, September 21, 1997, Day One:

> Lord, today I begin. I don't know how long this will last. You, O Lord, know my fears. I am painfully aware of my weaknesses. Hear me and give me

grace to seek You. Let this be the first day of a new life of prayer and intimacy with You.

Can you see that hand beckoning to you? Can you feel the Father tugging at your heart, asking you to come and begin, or begin again? Don't let fear of failure hold you back. I'm not asking you to make the same commitment I made at that conference so many years ago, but I am asking you this:

Are you willing to settle for a relationship with the Father that is "a mile wide and an inch deep," or do you want to experience God beyond the shallows? Can you see that hand? Say yes to it. Begin.

About the Author

Dave Jacobs was a pastor for twenty-eight years before retiring in 2006 and founding Small Church Pastor, an organization that provides encouragement, coaching, consulting, and resources for pastors and leaders of churches of all sizes, but with a focus on smaller churches. Dave and his wife, Ellen, have been married for thirty-five years and live out in the country in the beautiful Rogue Valley of southern Oregon.

You can reach Dave at:
dave@smallchurchpastor.com
www.smallchurchpastor.com
www.davejacobs.net

Notes

Introduction

[1] Philip Wagner, "The Secret Pain of Pastors," *ChurchLeaders.com*, http://www.churchleaders.com/pastors/pastor-articles/167379-philip-wagner-secret-pain-of-pastors.html.

[2] José María Arancedo, prologue to *Open Mind, Faithful Heart: Reflections on Following Jesus*, by Pope Francis (New York: The Crossroad Publishing Company, 2013), xviii.

Chapter 1

[3] Steve Ogne and Tim Roehl, *TransforMissional Coaching: Empowering Leaders in a Changing Ministry World* (Nashville, TN: B&H Publishing Group, 2008), 171.

[4] Stephen D. Summerell, *Overcoming Obstacles to Spiritual Formation in the Lives of Vineyard Pastors* (Azusa, CA: Azusa Pacific University, 2007).

[5] Eugene H. Peterson, *The Contemplative Pastor: Returning to the Art of Spiritual Direction* (Grand Rapids, MI: Wm. B. Eerdmans Publishing Co., 1993), 17, 19, 23. First published 1989.

[6] Henri Nouwen, Reprinted by permission. *Turn My Mourning Into into Dancing: Finding Hope in Hard Times*, Henri Nousen, 2001 (Thomas Nelson Inc. Nashville, TN: Thomas Nelson, Inc., 2004.), 8. First published 2001. All rights reserved.

[7] Richard Foster, *Celebration of Discipline: The Path to Spiritual Growth, Revised Edition* (New York, NY: HarperCollins Publishers, 19781998), 27. First published 1978. Also, reproduced by permission of Hodder and Stoughton. Copyright © revised edition 1989 by Richard Foster. Richard Foster, *Celebration of Discipline, Revised Edition*

Chapter 2

[8] Eugene H. Peterson, *Five Smooth Stones for Pastoral Work* (Grand Rapids, MI: Wm. B. Eerdmans Publishing Co., 1992), 62. First published 1980.

[9] Foster, *Celebration of Discipline*, 15. Also, reproduced by permission of Hodder and Stoughton. Copyright © revised edition 1989 by Richard Foster. Richard Foster, *Celebration of Discipline, Revised Edition*

[10] A. W. Tozer, *The Purpose of Man: Designed to Worship*, ed. James L. Snyder (Ventura, CA: Regal, 2009), 16.

[11] Nouwen, Reprinted by permission. *Turn My Mourning into Dancing*, 41.

Chapter 3

[12] Kent Carlson and Mike Lueken, *Renovation of the Church: What Happens When a Seeker Church Discovers Spiritual Formation* (Downers Grove, IL: InterVarsity Press, 2011), 10, 76-77.

Chapter 5

[13] Samuel D. Rima, *Rethinking the Successful Church: Finding Serenity in God's Sovereignty* (Ada, MI: Baker Books, 2002), 168.

[14] Rima, *Rethinking the Successful Church*, 163.

[15] Ibid., 48.

[16] Ibid., 173.

Chapter 8

[17] Richard Foster, *Celebration of Discipline, Revised Edition* (New York, NY: HarperCollins Publishers, 1978), 1. Also, reproduced by permission of Hodder and Stoughton. Copyright © revised edition 1989 by Richard Foster. Richard Foster, *Celebration of Discipline, Revised Edition*

[18] Robert Inchausti, ed., *Seeds*, by Thomas Merton (Boston, MA: Shambhala Publications, Inc., 2002), 1.

Chapter 9

[19] Henri Nouwen, *Our Greatest Gift: A Meditation on Dying and Caring* (New York: HarperOne, 2009), 1. First published 1994.

[20] Nouwen, Reprinted by permission. *Turn My Mourning iInto Dancing*, Henri Nousen, 2001 (Thomas Nelson Inc. Nashville, Tennessee.) 41-42. All rights reserved.

[21] Peterson, *Five Smooth Stones for Pastoral Work*, 61-62.

[22] Thomas Merton, *A Year with Thomas Merton: Daily Meditations from His Journals*, ed. Jonathan Montaldo (San Francisco: HarperCollins Publishers, 2004), 8.

Chapter 13

[23] Fred Smith Sr., *Breakfast with Fred*, (Ventura, CA: Regal Books, 2007), 115, 114.

[24] Francis Bacon, Essays no. 50, 'Of Studies', 1625

[25] Thomas Merton, *Turning Toward the World: The Journals of Thomas Merton Volume Four 1960-1963*, ed. Victor A. Kramer (San Francisco: HarperSanFrancisco, 1996), 149.

[26] Thomas Merton, *Entering the Silence: The Journals of Thomas Merton Volume Two 1941-1952*, ed. Jonathan Montaldo (San Francisco: HarperSanFrancisco, 1996), 435.

Chapter 15

[27] Ursula King, *Christian Mystics* (Mahwah, NJ: HiddenSpring, 2001), 249.

31875571R00087

Made in the USA
Charleston, SC
28 July 2014